Tom Raworth was born in 1938 and grew up in South East London. He left school at 16 out of boredom and worked at a variety of jobs, frequenting all-night jazz clubs and playing piano in a short-lived jazz combo. In 1965 he founded Goliard Press with Barry Hall, publishing many leading British and American poets of that era. In later years he has read his poetry widely in Britain, Europe and the United States. His work has been translated into French, Dutch, Swedish, Italian, Hungarian and Romanian. Amongst his books are: *The Relation Ship*

Books are to be returned on or before the last date below.

D1462833

LIBREX —

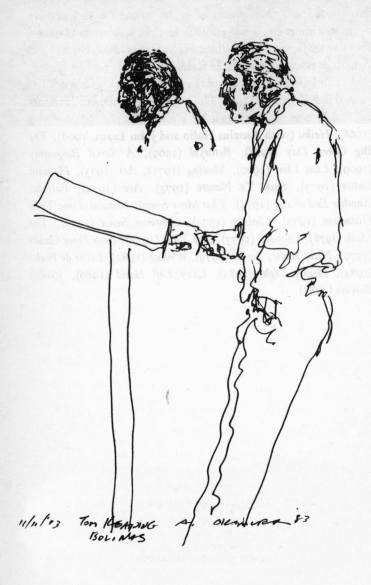

TOM RAWORTH

Tottering State

Selected Poems 1963–1987

**PALADIN
GRAFTON BOOKS**

A Division of the Collins Publishing Group

LONDON GLASGOW
TORONTO SYDNEY AUCKLAND

Paladin
Grafton Books
A Division of the Collins Publishing Group
8 Grafton Street, London W1X 3LA

A Paladin UK Paperback Original 1988

An earlier version of this book was published in
the United States of America by *The Figures* 1984
Copyright © Tom Raworth 1984, 1988
Frontispiece by Arthur Okamura

ISBN 0-586-08705-2

Printed and bound in Great Britain by
Collins, Glasgow

Set in Granjon

All rights reserved. No part of this publication may
be reproduced, stored in a retrieval system, or
transmitted, in any form, or by any means, electronic,
mechanical, photocopying, recording or otherwise,
without the prior permission of the publishers.

This book is sold subject to the condition that it
shall not, by way of trade or otherwise, be lent,
re-sold, hired out or otherwise circulated
without the publisher's prior consent in any
form of binding or cover other than that in
which it is published and without a similar
condition including this condition being imposed
on the subsequent purchaser.

As their selection, this book is for
Val Raworth
John Barrell
Kit Robinson
and
Geoffrey Young

من به عادة لا يتركها

The poems in this book appear in approximately the order they were written, rather than that in which they were published. The following people, at different times during twenty-five years, liked something I had written enough to offer to publish it. They gave their time, their energy and often the little money they had: I thank them – and the editors of the magazines in which some of the poems were first printed – here.

David Ball (*Pleasant Butter*, 1972; *Cloister*, 1975)

Asa Benveniste (*Haiku*, 1968; *The Big Green Day*, 1968; *Lion Lion*, 1970; *Act*, 1973)

Paul Brown (*Heavy Light*, 1981/84; *Lazy Left Hand*, 1986)

George Butterick (*That More Simple Natural Time Tone Distortion*, 1975)

Bob & Eileen Callahan (*A Serial Biography*, 1977)

Raymond DiPalma (*Tracking*, 1972)

Paul Green (*Tractor Parts*, 1984)

Barry Hall (*The Relation Ship*, 1966/69; *Moving*, 1971; *Ace*, 1974)

Alastair Johnson and Frances Butler (*The Mask*, 1976; *Logbook*, 1977; *Nicht Wahr, Rosie?*, 1979)

Stuart and Deirdre Montgomery (*A Serial Biography*, 1969)

Wendy Mulford (*Four Door Guide*, 1979)

Elaine Randell (*Bolivia: Another End of Ace*, 1974)

John Robinson (*Back to Nature*, 1973)

Leslie Scalapino (*Visible Shivers*, 1988)

David Southern (*Catacoustics/Lèvre de Poche*, 1984/89)

Richard Tabor (*Sky Tails*, 1978)

Holbrook Teter and Michael Myers (*Sic Him, Oltorf!*, 1974; *Common Sense*, 1976)

Geoffrey Young (*Ace*, 1977; *Writing*, 1982; *Tottering State*, 1984)

The four poems 'At Maximum Zero', 'What Do You Say?', 'A Most Cold', and 'What You Got?' are from a series of 're-translations' of three poems which had been published in Hungarian, a language I neither speak nor read.

CONTENTS

Tottering State

WAITING

she made it a
noise
    entering the room
as he sat holding
a cigarette   grey
smoke &
     blue
he was too   sound
of children moving so
much outside he wrote
small she
spoke he
cut a pack of tarot cards page
of (shall we go she said) pentacles re
versed meaning prodigality
dissipation liberality un
favourable news

BUT I DON'*LOVE*

but i don'*love*
you she said   there were
drops of sweat
                on the receiver
warm sun the sky
on the horizon turquoise   a faint
haze
      red trains crossed the bridge

they played war forecast music   as they
walked down the hill the brown
girls passed
                driving their own cars

the tree had not been climbed
they disturbed the dirt   it grew
like a ladder
from below the sound of water on the leaves

but she said you stroked her
hair she said she is like a
cow you are so
obvious

the gardens of the houses go down
to the stream   there are a few
allotments the path
was overgrown   they walked single file
under the north circular road   the tunnel
chalk inscriptions latest dated 1958
                                no sound

from the cars overhead
                              the lake
dark red flowers   green
scum no
current a red
ball
      stationary in the middle

THE OTHERS

she said nothing
leaned on the stone bridge   the wind
howled in my ear, pause
between the dropping
of the record and the music

dust   the wind   the streets
already in shadow

we walked   someone
playing the piano in a tiled room

oh
said her mother a
mister dante called you
                              beatrice

SING

a certain
drum beat   it is that of
skin

the button found
still
    vibrating

produce
the body   this
small thing?

i hold, here
only the fat remaining   sound
of a fingertip lighter
without ring   it

is the pressure of air i
don't remember

YOU WERE WEARING BLUE

the explosions are nearer this evening
the last train leaves for the south
at six   tomorrow
the announcements will be in a different language

i chew the end of a match
the tips of my finger and thumb are sticky

i will wait at the station and you
will send a note, i
will read it
                it will be raining

                our shadows in the electric light

when i was eight they taught me *real*
writing
        to join up the letters

listen you said i
preferred to look

                at the sea. everything stops there at strange angles

only the boats spoil it
making you focus further

WEDDING DAY

noise of a ring sliding onto a finger

supposing he *did* say that?
we came by the front
sea fog twisting light above the pebbles
towards the cliffs towards the sea

i made this pact, intelligence
shall not replace intuition, sitting here
my hand cold on the typewriter
flicking the corner of the paper. he

came from the toilet wearing
a suit, people
didn't recognise him, down the length
of corridor. the room
was wooden, sunlight   we stood in a half circle

noise of two cine-cameras

i wonder what's wrong with her
face, she said, because
there's nothing wrong with it really   i
inhabit a place just to the left of that phrase. from

a bath the father took champagne later
whiskey. through the window we watched the frigate's
orange raft drifting to shore

i mean if you're taking *that*

attitude
        we rode in a train watching the dog move

noise of a bicycle freewheeling downhill

ANNIVERSARY

the train runs, trying to reach the end of the darkness

for the time that is left, if you will permit
i will recant and withdraw from my insecurity
see, i give you this bullet with my name on it
how neatly it fits your mouth. certainly
the words that trigger it are unknown to both of us
as yet. i have worn channels in the air of this room
that are mine, a way of progressing
from desk to door to table. just now not
thinking, i touched the tip of my cigarette
to the head of a moth walking by my paper knife
and realised only when it spun and spun and fluttered
what i had done. a comet. the patterns in the sky

the six of us move in the night
each carrying a different coloured torch

MY FACE IS MY OWN, I THOUGHT

morning   he had gone
down to the village   a figure
she still recognised from his walk

nothing
        he had explained
is won by arguing   things are changed
only by power
                and cunning   she still sat
meaning to ask what
did you say   ?   echo in her ears

he might just have finished speaking   so
waiting and
                taking the scissors
began to trim off the baby's fingers

THREE

smell of shit when i lift him he knocks the book from my hand
i hold him up she pulls at my leg the other comes in with a
    book
he gives me his book picks up my book she pulls at his arm
    the other
is pulling my hair i put him down he pulls at my leg she
has taken my book from him and gives it to me i give him his
    book
give her an apple touch the other's hair and open the door

they go down the hall all carrying something

MORNING

she came in laughing his
shit's blue and red today those
wax crayons he ate last night   you know
he said eating the cake the
first thing nurses learn
is how to get rid of an erection say
you get one whilst they're shaving
you, they give it a knock like
this, he flicked his hand and
waved it down she
screamed, the baby stood in the doorway
carrying the cat
in the cat's mouth a bird fluttered

SIX DAYS

monday

i was alone then looking at the picture of a child with
    the same birthday
a key turned in another lock there was a noise through
    the window
the cigarette made noises like a cheap firework
in the ruins of so much love in this room i must leave
    something
the morning was sunny it is easier to die on such a day
    a blister under your foot and easier still to
    mention it
a need to explain this and a french dictionary i worried
    how to carry the bottle in my case with only a cork
sweat dripped from my nose in the picture a man wrote in
    a room behind a peacock there were two clocks in
    the room and two watches twenty nine bottles four
    of them my own
i wanted to share everything and keep myself it would
    not work
on the door a drawing of a lion in this room on the
    mirror in soap it said *write*
the plane was always level and the moon dipped

i had cleaned the room all my taste had gone the whiskey
    tasted like milk chocolate
i had bought all the books for my friends my shoulder
    still ached from the case i would be carrying
    more back
a leaf i had found and given to her all green with four
    brown eyes

five years ago i had stood on those steps the next month
        she was wearing a white dress the car was late i
        combed my hair in a window in the tube it was still
        summer i
was and still am addicted to self-pity

a handkerchief to my face and the blood dried i would have
        left it
the shelter smelled of earth there was a shovel inside to
        dig yourself out nine paving stones in the path
a tall brown girl in jeans who came up the steps of the
        bridge something about rhythm the line and breathing
motions

tuesday

the whiskey began to taste like whiskey the cigarettes
        still made noises
i had not noticed that beside the peacock was a quieter
        bird in front of it a dish and through the window
        a countryside
day of daniel there had been noise and i fitted a lock
        to my door
a long while ago i read silone 'i came home,' he said,
        when he was able to continue
'and told my parents the doctor had advised me to return
        to my native climate.'

so wrote to you this letter
my jacket was wet from the window it was all grey except
        for one green tree by the pantheon
there was a sound of water in the streets the americans
        wore white trousers and red shirts
i counted my money it was tuesday i ate salt because i

was still sweating
then the rain stopped and it was all white the tree
    vanished there were red tiles

he was five and he said to me why are you not nice look
    i gave you that calendar
i bought him a toy french car every year he looked after
    them and never lost the tyres
i was aware of having a family the policemen all had
    mustaches
bought oranges and chocolate, bread, wine and coca-cola
soda à base d'extraits végétaux
i could not write anything without repeatedly using i
    someday i would get over it
my teeth ached from politeness it felt like october '62

they take up the cobbles and re-lay them in the same
    pattern
they wear blue jackets and blue trousers and blue caps
the stones are grey underneath is sand
they do this every year and wash the public buildings

let me tell you about the needles i said
isn't it the truth? you find them everywhere. even in
    bay city.

wednesday

today it is warm and the americans wear blue nylon
    raincoats
it is with a 'c' she said shall i wait outside a skin
    formed on the soup
there were brown leaves already it was only july
and between the grey stones drifted green buds dead
    fish in the river

i have no love and therefore i have liberty it said on
        the wall and underneath with my key i scratched
        'lincoln'
pas lincoln she said bien sûr i answered an elastic
        band floated by
there are statues of all the queens of france she said
        there was cream on her nose
my throat is sorry do not go down those alleys at night
        there are thieves and murderers
this cinema is the biggest in europe maurice thorez est
        mort
enregistrez un disque a way to send letters

when we left ravensbruck she said we could not stop
        laughing and joking for half an hour

thursday

in the musée national d'art moderne there are three
    modigliani paintings two sculptures a copy of matisse's
    book 'jazz' five statues by germaine richier a plaster
    construction to walk inside statues by arp a restaurant
    and a reconstruction of brancusi's studio
it was half past three the girl in the american express
    looked sad and shook her head
everyone was kissing it was like a commercial for paris
on a newsstand i read in the guardian about the strike
    they said at the british council library mr ball
    has left?
in les lettres nouvelles june 1960 i read requiem spontané
    pour l'indien d'amérique with a footnote saying little
    richard – jazzman célèbre

from a corner of his studio the stairs went up to nowhere
there was a blowlamp and an axe a pile of wood
i looked at myself in brancusi's mirror and it was round

friday

they were painting the outside of david's house white
30 rue madame i would not have recognised it
posters say tous à la mutualité avec pierre poujade
pigeon shit runs into apollinaire's left eye

the light through her sunglasses makes her eye look
      bruised
other pigeons coo a sound of water splashing men shovel
      the leaves as the yacht is thrown it moves
a blue balloon the carts stand there are cigarette
      ends in the gravel
wearing a black dress with green spots gold sandals
      an indian girl walks through the gardens reading a
      music manuscript

on the steps at night five spaniards singing *la bamba*
long r's and a noise like a cricket
she moves another chair to rest her feet

one spot of nail polish on her stocking little song
      you have been pushing behind my eyes all day

saturday

a letter came i felt very strange at gloucester road she
      said after you went and i had kisses from four people
i wanted to be there people move into church a door slams
      the car moves

i could not say i tried
i said i
could not   people have hair on the backs of their hands

26

what did we eat we ate sausage a stew
of onions tomatoes and courgettes below in the square
    they played boules
six men and a fair brown woman in a black dress

emptiness a taste of brass the holes in my head filled
    with warm sand
a scar beneath her left eye yellow bruises inside her
    elbows
in the *marais* we bought sweet cakes in the heat without
    shirts there were still tattooed numbers
birds walk inside the dry pool the flowers are dark
    and even
on the wooden floor the cup broke quickly calvados a
    faint smell of apples

looking at the etruscan statues in the louvre there is
    a green patina on my hands my expression has taken
    its final shape
everything becomes modern inside these cases there is
    nothing without touching

children crawl under the glass   things are reflected
    several times

A PRESSED FLOWER

and now there is a movement another
child   i am unable to help you
at all times — irritated when you clutch my hand now
still spellbound when you talk

there is no decomposition
                              at the same moment
evening
     only the ground is dark, the sky still palest blue, and
your grandfather whom i also love is perhaps dying
these first weeks of the new year   because
you are me i tear at you *how*
can i channel it?   the children
develop my faintly irritated voice   they wave their hands

at the other end of the line i say
there is no answer   but the room there
is filled with people looking at the phone

HAIKU

now the melody
in the pattern of shadows
one shadow behind

slow cello music
pushing the velvet armchair
as the rain comes down

time under pressure
dawn, and the green butterflies
crossing the ice-cap

tracked down by process
inside the dentist's peephole
, but i fixed him good

spinnets of silver
one hair caught between my teeth
whose? i've been away

the wax filtered sounds
earth where imagination
spreads a boned circle

a mould of eyelids
under the singing emblem
cough, and he dropped them

the problem of form
within this limitation
he drops a sylla

ORRERY

seigneur the words pushed further
baby the whole tingSOO much
it might belong there, it did belong there, that piano
the corners of the room pushed her
fingers into her ears, mad woman
the carnations of the mad woman, her mother

COLLAPSIBLE

behind the calm famous faces knowledge of what crimes?
rain on one window showing the wind's direction

a jackdaw collecting phrases "it's a chicken!"
nothing lonelier than hearing your own pop in another country

        whose face with bandages was singing
her breath always only half an inch from the corner of my eye

NOW THE PINK STRIPES

now the pink stripes, the books, the clothes you wear
in the eaves of houses i ask whose land it is

an orange the size of a melon rolling slowly across the field
where i sit at the centre in an upright coffin of five panes of glass

there is no air   the sun shines
and under me you've planted a quick growing cactus

YOU'VE RUINED MY EVENING/
YOU'VE RUINED MY LIFE

i would be eight people and then the difficulties vanish
only as one i contain the complications
in a warm house roofed with the rib-cage of an elephant
i pass my grey mornings re-running the reels
and the images are the same but the emphasis shifts
the actors bow gently to me and i envy them
their repeated parts, their constant presence in that world

i would be eight people each inhabiting the others' dreams
walking through corridors of glass framed pages
telling each other the final lines of letters
picking fruit in one dream and storing it in another
only as one i contain the complications
and the images are the same, their constant presence in that world
the actors bow gently to each other and envy my grey mornings

i would be eight people with the rib-cage of an elephant
picking fruit in a warm house above actors bowing
re-running the reels of my presence in this world
the difficulties vanish and the images are the same
eight people, glass corridors, page lines repeated
inhabiting grey mornings roofed with my complications
only as one walking gently storing my dream

HOT DAY AT THE RACES

in the bramble bush shelley slowly eats a lark's heart
we've had quite a bit of rain since you were here last
raw silk goes on soft ground (result of looking in the form book)
two foggy dell seven to two three ran
crouched, the blood drips on his knees
and horses pass

shelley knows where the rails end
did i tell you about the blinkered runners?

shelley is waiting with a crossbow for his rival, the jockey
all day he's watched the races from his bush
now, with eight and a half furlongs to go
raw silk at least four lengths back disputing third place
he takes aim

and horses pass

his rival, the jockey, soars in the air
and falls.   the lark's beak neatly pierces his eye

LOVE POEM

there have been so many other men in my pause life
don't be frightened pause it's just my pause way
(he's going to force his *way* into her *life* — well folks
that's why we came out here to the free west

section 2

i've never said you were unattractive.   that's another
distortion.   i've just said unattractive to *me* at this *time*
certainly men would be attracted to you but let them have six
years of *this* sort of thing then see what they'd be like

3.

"he speaks for all of us"

4.   continuing

how there are some nauseating actresses who *must* at some stage
        of their careers have played cripples (once i tried
        to let a smile be my umbrella.   i got awful wet)

on to 5

like the balinese say 'we have no art, we just do everything as
            well as possible'

6. (and approaching the bend)

where is the thing i want to hold? the heroin i take is you and
        that is sentimental.   which is not sex but something more
        subversive

7.

too far. look back. you've missed the point

8. the end

yes the sun i love *came* through the window
and the last rays were *in* the park

NORTH AFRICA BREAKDOWN

it was my desert army. no fuss. no incidents.
you just have to be patient with it. take your time.
a child leaving a dirty black car (with running boards)
wearing a thick too large overcoat: grainy picture.
each night round the orange dial of the wireless.

or innocence. oh renaissance.
a dutch island where horses pull to launch the lifeboat.
we are specifically ordered that there shall be no fast cars.
where can we go when we retire?

it was their deduction we were afraid of
so shall we try just once more?
nothing is too drastic when it comes to your son, eleanor.

and nothing works in this damn country.
no, it's not a bit like home.

AH THE POETRY OF MISS PARROT'S FEET
DEMONSTRATING THE TANGO

we were leaving on a journey by slow aeroplane
that was the weapon you had picked for our duel
flying above a gigantic playing-card (the five of spades)
from one corner to the other – our goal the gilt edge

this is a pretense (i quote your note), a cut, take the short way
because justice is what the victim of law knows is right
your stockings rasped in the silence, the engine stopped
and i wished it had been a ten of clubs with more landing space

it was a game in the air, flock wallpaper in the cockpit
outside feathers grew from metal, flapped, and we began to climb
from the mechanical smoothness to the motion of a howdah
i picked up the card, removed my goggles, and began to dance

SHOES

shoes come from leather leather
comes from cows come from milk no
no milk comes from cows come
from shoes baby shoes
                come
from there to here hear
the shoes of blind children shoes
shuffling tripping a blind child falls into a cement mixer
a deaf child is crushed by the ambulance racing to the
    blind child who is the child of some dumb man who
    makes shoes

that evening he cries over a piece of leather stained with milk
the tear marks make a pattern he tries to read to read
he wants to cut the leather into the shape of a gingerbread man

he wants very much to have his child back
to ride on the cows back

THESE ARE NOT CATASTROPHES I WENT OUT OF MY WAY TO LOOK FOR

corners of my mouth sore
i keep licking them, drying them with the back of my hand
bitten nails but three i am growing
skin frayed round the others white flecks on them all

no post today, newspapers and the children's
comic, i sit
in the lavatory reading heros the spartan
and the iron man

flick ash in the bath trying to hit the plughole
listen to the broom outside examine
new pencil marks on the wall, a figure four

the shadows, medicines, a wicker
laundry basket lid pink with toothpaste

between my legs i read

       levi stra
        origina
      quality clo

             leaning too far forward
into the patch of sunlight

TOM TOM

awakening this morning by the baobab tree
the bright colours of my clothes fading
catarrh a slow trickle in the back of my throat

the animals whose names i know only in dialect
in this place as the day grows and the air vibrates

eyes nose and mouth the dark green of our statues
face of an ape the symbol of justice and death gone

gone chaka the welder of a thousand tribes

GOT ME

did you ever fall asleep making love in a rocking chair?
i did, and i remember every minute. that's really
when i began to drink, then i drank again, and finally
    some more
then i started to hang little heavy baskets of drink on
    my thoughts to keep them down
which was about the same time i wrote my famous
    corrected poem, you may remember it

~~GOT ME~~

~~did you ever~~ fall asleep ~~making love in a~~ rocking ~~chair?~~
~~i did,~~ and ~~i~~ remember every minute. ~~that's really~~

THE BLOWN AGENT

her blue gown is taking the smoke
the dust on the hem of her blue gown
blue gown – that's nice

in the low corridors of the old school   that smell
and her blue gown, poor dog
all those years the cake had lasted
we collected the dust in a matchbox

immobile   the petals   the horizon   the the
lonely in the radio and no room to click my fingers
over my head   moon   moon

on a bicycle, after the cars had left, her blue gown, going

GITANES

where do all the cigarette ends go?   the world should be
    littered with them
i reach for one like an oxygen mask when the trip gets bumpy
sometimes i smoke 5,000 a day, alternating between white
    and yellow
(i also drink cider and breed lettuce
here on my small farm printing fake photographs of my
    parents)

the ivy has grown over my inscription
lines spread from the nose, greasy, across the forehead
she's breaking up!   i try to block them with cigarettes
filling the wrinkles with ash, smoothing it over, applying
    make-up

no, that was in '38.   i'm heading that way fast
matches all gone i vainly rub the end on my bristles
friction should do it, no, that was douglas fairbanks jnr. on
    t.v.

did you see him?   i almost smoked my ear
here, stepping off the pavement, damn fool, i bet he'd been
    smoking
all those books under their arms.   a rhythm of footsteps.
    sheets blowing
with cigarette burns.   and they don't flush down the toilet
    first time

well girls, *shave* those books from under your armpits
she did, and there was a small hole from which she pulled
a never ending cigarette, yellow, white, yellow, white

so we went into the labyrinth and killed the minotaur,
    holding on
but coming back, half-way, we found it burning
and a gnome had eaten the ash.   puff puff, puff puff

ORATORIO

who came first?
as joseph asked that question the ball went into the pocket
erything was a gamble and music began softly in the background
both with amnesia
again the violins
it was possible then
that they were really there
only a few feet from the main line
hold back the credits
joseph took a leaf and kissed it
he looked this way and that
around the circle
but the diamonds in her hair were soft bird droppings

SARABAND

behind the trees
where i can not hear the voices
inside the tent
its tasselled curtains and deep carpets
balance the candle against the grey image
ah
i tell you
a banjo
here miles below the city
among the roots of trees
smaller than an ant
the bridge is swinging

NOCTURNE

or is life cold?
in the early hours as the fire is dying
dance
take another bottle
bunch up the pillow
to sit staring with only a blanket
it's time the flying saucer left
my thoughts like grease around you
as you swim across

VARIATIONS

do you remember a hill, miranda?
and the times we'd sit on the cool veranda
talking of films was it bande a
part from you there is no-one miranda
and just about here i had planned to
change the rhyme
just one more time
a reverse.   last line

miranda. a hill. i remember. do you?

THE UNIVERSITY OF ESSEX

1. gone to lunch back in five minutes

night closed in on my letter of resignation
out in the square one of my threads had broken loose
the language i used was no and no
while the yellow still came through, the hammer and the drills

occasionally the metabolism alters
and lines no longer come express
waiting for you what muscles work me
which hold me down below my head?

it is a long coat and a van on the horizon
a bird that vanishes   the arabic
i learn from observation is how to break the line

genius creates surprises: the metropolitan
police band singing 'bless this house'

as the filmed extractor fans inflate the house with steam

2. walking my back home

the wind
is the wind
is a no-vo-cain band

and the footstep
                echoes

i
have conjured *people*

3. ah, it all falls into place

when it was time what he had left became a tile
bodies held shaped by the pressure of air
were clipped to his attention by their gestures

my but we do have powerful muscles
each of us equal to gravity

or sunlight that forces our shadows
into the pieces of a fully interlocking puzzle

4. good morning he whispered

the horrors of the horses are the crows
the bird flies past the outside the library
many heels have trapped the same way
he tolls, he lapsed with the light from so many trees

check the pattern swerves with the back
the tree that holds the metal spiral staircase swings
aloft the hand removes a book and checked it
for death by glasses or the angle food descends

5. the broadcast

she turns me on she turns on me
that the view from the window is a lake

and silent cars are given the noise of flies dying in the heat
of the library   the grass outside goes brown
in my head behind my glasses behind the glass in the precinct
thus, too, they whisper in museums and banks

ON THE THIRD FLOOR AND A HALF

grains on a spoon
the barrage balloons
echo in the bay

a polite gesture with the tray
to let her pass
away with gentle movements

stirring into the foam
a train where they have changed
the destination plates

HOW CAN YOU THROW IT ALL AWAY
ON THIS RAGTIME?

the sound track cut flickered to the past connection
inspiration came on to her like at coffee

the twelth period begins with one lizard
cold blades of itzcoliuhqui

he can not move in clothes that are not his
trigger to many connections

of course the key slips through the grating
trust marginal thoughts

some like shoes will fit
the will to make out

GOING TO THE ZOO

shapes that come in the night
three tulips through my window
hair brushed in the next room

the black panther extends his leg
here is the site of the battle of maldon
mum ee mum ee mum ee

the order is all things happening now
no way down through you float in the density
so sensitively turned on the animals

LION LION

the happy hunters are coming back
eager to be captured, to have someone unravel the knot
but nobody can understand the writing
in the book they found in the lions' lair

CLAUDETTE COLBERT BY BILLY WILDER

run, do not walk, to the nearest exit
spain, or is democracy doomed?
we regret that due to circumstances beyond our control
we are unable to bring you the cambridge crew trials

if you're counting my eyebrows
i can tell you there are two
i took your letter out and read it to the rabbits

describe the sinking ship
describe the sea at night
he lived happily ever after in the café magenta

how to preserve peaches
they're counting on you for intimate
personal stuff about hitler and his gang
it's a chance i wouldn't miss for anything in the
wait in holland for
instance watching the windmills
that's more than flash gordon ever did

all those bugles blowing
in the ears of a confused liberal
so long
pretty woman
wake me up at the part where he claims milwaukee

THE LEMON TREE

a.

across the bare plain dogs pass in the sun
pepsi-colon say the signs and breakW-ater
the hard lacquer of the only cypress that stands
in the glare of old bones, the houses made from them

b.

there is no way to stop crying into my cigarette
tears the taste of medlar fruit
of rinsed saucers no way the tiles
are coming true

c.

across the street smooth girls behind their glasses have it made
but in the end what gift do they give
guarded so carefully soaked every day in sweat
powdered, perfumed, exchange, cambio, wechsel

d.

who had the pylon and the rest
of all that over the caves on the hill
without speaking german or clicking or
hearing the children leave school dancing

hearing the cloth cameras the silent
roar of the famous lions i obviously
came all this way to see

e.

i am learning spanish
but in granada we buy before we try
tiene gracia he said: gracia (f) grace,
attraction; favour; kindness; jest,
witticism; pardon, mercy; pleasant
manner; obligingness, willingness.
(pl.) thanks, thank you

f.

it was only glass, albert, and the cyclist was an illusion
hello, albert, in my glass, in my room, i sleep in your tree

JUNGLE BOOK

stranger. a curious hand touches the snow raising pigeons

they want us to compete so they need only read 'the best'
next line
this beautifully carved hand is for scratching the ice to attract
    the seal's attention

come, take my place in the long hibernation dream of the hamste

LEMURES

1.
lovat on the cancered hand
lemniscus – or was it franz lehar?
i can't consult it any more

2.
it's all coming back to me, thanks
that skill again now
and in nahuatl

COME BACK, COME BACK,
O GLITTERING AND WHITE!

life is against the laws of nature, this we know
from nothing bangs again the heart each time
shadow and light push back across the lawn
the grass that feels them both of equal weight

and memory keeps going, clutching the straws
of similarity in taste or scent
flickering in laminates or spiralling through tracks
the perfume of you was and keeps on going

DEAR SIR, FLYING SAUCERS! FLYING
SAUCERS! FLYING SAUCERS!

he is taking a glass but the hand of his shadow touches the
        door
the day has warmed the pebbles   now why is this?
his passport   his papers   the letter of credit
says people are born in high places that empty

there is no imagery to explain this new feeling
outside the range of sound and sight   he worries about
the other three   packing, packing, his head
turning over the surface still dreams of the water

SOUTH AMERICA

he is trying to write down a book he wrote years ago in his head
an empty candlestick on the windowsill   each day
of his life he wakes in paris to the sound of vivaldi in summer
and finds the space programme fascinating since he still doesn't
    know
how radio works   as in the progress of art the aim is finally
to make rules the next generation can break more cleverly
    this
morning he has a letter from his father saying "i have set my face
as a flint against a washbasin in the lavatory. it seems to me
almost too absurd and sybaritic" how they still don't know
where power lies or how to effect change
he clings to a child's book called 'all my things' which says:
ball (a picture of a ball) drum (a picture of a drum) book (a
    picture of a book)

all one evening he draws on his left arm with felt-tipped pens
an intricate pattern   feels how the pain does give protection
and in the morning finds faint repetitions on the sheets, the inside
of his thigh, his forehead   reaching this point
he sees that he has written pain for paint   and it works better

PROVENCE

1.

in the morning there is opera, *faïencerie*
dance dance to break off the filter

singing songs he could not play on his teeth

edge edge dance dance
in the morning to opera along the cliff road

his teeth were the filter and filled
with gold

that would not take an edge the bark
whittled whittled into a tooth pick in mourning

2.

so i rode to my lady's castle
horse stepping gently through screaming vines
the noise of our train filled the valley

my lady was sowing
sweep sweep of her arm
white seed slashed like water

oh my lady is brown, red
and crumbling on the green velour
smear of my seed   horse   stop

3.
the tape of my mother does not have that high pitch
the ape swung from the high tree

crash of the door took my mother under the ape's arm
she spun over my daughter in the brown dust

4.
stone or heart, the ashes surround my plate
the horse i ride on is dappled with leaves
that would break the skin. i wait for the sound of a car
in the noise of the valley bringing a spoiled gift

KING OF THE SNOW

the hunchback child gets finally to me
in sewage washing oranges towards the cave
she drifts, eating a yellow jelly cake

in a dry ravine the bones make orange dust
that wind drifts into words   the lemon tree
edges towards the child towards its children

a lemon bursts   the orange pus congeals
two elements that form a crooked hand
of bones   that gives the child a message

CHANCER

others turn off and now he rides the right straight way
the shadows uniform in their direction

in the down of D., among strangers
he asked to be going home, silently

one inch from the dark shore
bound to the ship as by a spell

this is a model of you i made
it contains thumbnail he thought went into the flames

STAG SKULL MOUNTED

9:00 p.m. May 1st. 1970

mounting a stag's skull remains
the province of a tiny man
who standing on a bolt peers
across eye socket rim at antlers
(the magnetic north) that are not his
heads   east again
upon a giant brown and white
saint bernard   which leads me
to today   obsessed by thoughts
of drowning in hot water in the dark
the hound's bark drifts
through trees in the night spring air
venus is out

8:00 p.m. May 5th. 1970

each evening the girl with a twisted spine
passes my window   as the weather warms
her dresses thin and shorten and useless pity
for the deformed and lonely leaves me
only this   i can not love her and her life
may be filled with warmth   i project my past
sadness on to all   the weight
of my thought of her misery may add
the grain that makes her sad   i should be dead
which is why today the roman wall
is not the stones the romans saw

11:08 a.m. May 7th. 1970

matthew coolly looks out from his comfortable seat in the suitcase. it is in the case that he travels with father unwin on the missions that require matthew to be minimised.

'found poem'

9:30 p.m. May 13th. 1970

the dog is at my feet
thin paper blocks my nose, round wax bumps over me
all magical instruments must be duplicated

the way is not a direction
but a smoothing of decay

i am a ping pong ball from face to face
idea to idea   and what i do
is a disservice
                to crystallise
the doorway   the landscape beyond
to withhold knowledge   to fashion
this from the jerks of thought and vision

12:15 p.m. May 19th. 1970

the government has explained the situation to us
pigeon in the beech tree

first a shoe shine then the whole wide world
Frank O'Hana

(the plane dropped in an effort

the government has explained the situation to us

pigeon in the beech tree
first a shoe shine then the whole wide world
Frank O'Hana

(the plane dropped in an effort

the government has explained the situation to us

pigeon in the beech tree first
a shoe shine then the whole wide world
Frank O'Hana

(the plane dropped in an effort

pigeon in the beech tree

the government has explained the situation to us
first a shoe shine then the whole wide world
Frank O'Hana

(the plane dropped in an effort

this vehicle is fitted with a hope anti jack knife device 1) 2) 3) 4)

9:30 p.m. May 24th. 1970

'and'   nobody
minds and covers blown
blossoms and leaves with love
zap zap zap zap 'and'?
the british rail insignia

'petrol burns'   'tomorrow's another day'

10:30 a.m. May 26th. 1970

wild elephants wouldn't drag me
in the rain gentle
men wear hats to the zoo today
i wake to read contracts
and smile that ron in his title
fused jerry lee lewis and john ashbery
with gracious goodness well
every packet bears the maker's signature
as it says on the box
of farrah's original harrogate toffee

(10:00 p.m. E.S.T. June 1st. 1970
just for the record
'great balls of fire!' was
something my mother and grand-
mother used to say (before
j.l. lewis, bless him).
                    love,
                    ron)

NOON *May 29th. 1970*

i can not find my way
back to myself i go
on trying

the sparkling games
flickering at the end of my youth

12:10 a.m. June 1st. 1970

the time is now

12:.256 a.m. June 1st. 1970

looking at my watch

11:42 a.m. June 2nd. 1970

opposites are timeless

it is the moment all time
is our selection

he had cultivated europe by the throat

9:37 a.m. June 3rd. 1970

this is my handwriting

1:31 p.m. June 5th. 1970

my up
is mind made

absolutely empty

now here comes thought thought
is laughing at language language
doesn't see the joke the joke
wonders why it takes so long

but it's friday
and it's a long way down

10:26 p.m. June 5th. 1970

word

10:59 p.m. June 5th. 1970

10:45 a.m. June 6th. 1970

word : a
a : the
the : the

in
   adequate language
        i love you

8:06 p.m. June 10th. 1970

poem

9:25 p.m. June 10th. 1970

poem
poem

7:19 p.m. June 29th. 1970

organic

7:21 p.m. June 29th. 1970

education

7:22 p.m. June 29th. 1970

laugh

7:40 p.m. June 29th. 1970

this trick doesn't work

would have explained it.   But asymptosy seems destined to leave it to Vespucci. The two styles fight even for my handwriting. Their chemicals, even, produce nothing more than wax in the ears and an amazing thirst. That seems to 'even' things, for those who regard it as a *balance,* or think the wind blows *one way.* The third day of our voyage was perilous. Multitudinous seas incarnadine. But the small craft that came out to meet us contained us and went sailing into the sunset, carrying only ten pages of my logbook (106, 291, 298, 301, 345, 356, 372, 399, 444 and 453), slightly charred by the slow still silent instant. And it was in that same instant (as everything is) that we recognised that in addition to our normal crew we had a stowaway – the author of *The Incredible Max* who, alone and unaided, had, on a long string, hauled the dinghy *Automatic Writing* (out from Deus ex Machinette) – or how else could he be explained? The eloquence of his moustache (you will understand) bulged neatly over and under his belt. He spoke of himself as ceaselessly sweeping up the leaves that fall from the trees. We tried to tell him about the other seasons – "Fall DOWN: Spring UP!" we made him repeat. "Fall DOWN: Sweep UP!" he added a beepbada beep beep. Or the pages. Or the faces in the trees' silhouettes at night. Around us was the countryside of *Whimsy* where, huddled around leaping orange fires, the natives let their cigarettes dangle unlit in their mouths, thinking only petrol or butane could light them. Stripping bark from each native to reveal our track we followed one string of dulcimer notes after another. Nothing is lost, or confused, in this country – not the PENGUIN ENGLISH DICTIONARY, nor the RED PEN, nor the YELLOW PEN WITH GREEN INK (Patent Applied For). At night in the forest we slept, listening to the creak of our future oars. "Let us," said one of the natives whose language we could speak, but imperfectly, "build from these trees a thing which we call a 'ship' – from the wood remaining I will show you how to make 'paper' – on this 'paper' (once we set sail) I shall show you how to 'write' (with a charred twig from the same tree) – and if your grandmother is with you, here's how we suck eggs." From the shore we watched the 'ship' approach us. We set sail in small craft to meet the strangers, pausing only to write pages 106, 291, 298, 301, 345, 356, 372, 399, 444 and 453 of the logbook, charring few words to each page to help the caps. I have been from one to another of my friends and I feel uneasy. I understand now that I have been dead ever since I can remember, and that in my wife I met another corpse. This is the way salt is made. We, the salt, get put on and in things. But we are our different taste. I am in Maine. Did your salt taste different today? What did you expect this to be? I am sodium – I realise now my fear and love of water. Chlorine. We have combined to save you from our separate dangers and become the sea. Sodium rode in the bus taking care not to sweat. In front of him the strange tracery ASHTRAY. To his left SAFETY EXIT – LIFT BAR – PULL RED CORD BELOW – PUSH WINDOW OPEN. He copied this tracery as the bus sped along the dotted line. Across a pale green metal bridge. To the left, grassy hillocks then pines. In the distance a black horse cropping. He counted four blue cars, one after another. The green tinted windows of the bus announced a storm. TS 306, another blue car, overtook the bus. This is MAINE, he told himself. And the selectors threw up 'an island off the rocky coast of Maine.' An exit road curved down. A truck called 'HEM-INGWAY' passed. What strange mutations will come from that grassy strip between the lanes – never walked on, fed by fumes, cans, paper, tobacco and typesetters who surely should, subtlety is only what you see looking around inside your head with a torch: beating your radar pulse there to yourself and back and describing the journey. No, that was something else. Red. Until the day I (   )ed that intelligence and intuition were the same, and passed through *that* fence. The word I choose so precisely becomes next day the key word in an advertising campaign to sell a brand of stockings, because the *word* means *what comes to mind first*. And as a 'writer' and 'artist' I should have sensed the direction of that word. As the renaissance painter should have sensed his picture on the packet around those same stockings with SIZE NINE printed across the detail which took him three days to paint. Because the stockings have always been there, and we are all USEFUL.... and the packet was one of the things for which he painted the picture. Like the con of ecology, which has been fed and fattened to keep your mind *off*. Buy CLEAN MACHINES. So long as we are all satisfied that matter cannot be destroyed it is a closed world. 'Art' says only "This is how I do this" – and a form can be used once only. "He planted that word twenty years ago so that its weight is now exactly right" – that's the message of 'culture', the real cold science. The last message to come through on the old transmitter was ELECTRICITY WILL STOP... and we have no way of knowing if the last word was message or punctuation. So before we think, have a programme to justify by now

I'm not going to make it to the lift in time, nor change my name, and the dialogue echoes off the walls of the set. It's the front room, and the queen's picture flickers into a limp book called Jimi Hendrix because all books are dead and we live where the edges overlap. The material is transparent, but the seam is already ripping down from Orion. And I am busily sweeping up the last few words in a country without an ear, whose artists are busy filling in the colours they've been allocated in the giant painting-by-numbers picture of themselves, because they think an interview with the man (now a physicist in Moscow) who was the boy on the Odessa Steps *makes a connection*. Full moon. High tide. Because it's all gesture, and nobody ever talked in words.

THE MOON UPOON THE WATERS

the green of days : the chimneys
alone : the green of days and the women
the whistle : the green of days : the feel of my nails
the whistle of me entering the poem through the chimneys
plural : i flow from the (each) fireplaces
the green of days : i barely reach the sill
the women's flecked nails : the definite article
i remove i and a colon from two lines above
the green of days barely reach the sill
i remove es from ices keep another i put the c here
the green of days barely reaches the sill
the beachball : dreaming 'the' dream
the dreamball we dance on the beach

gentlemen i am not doing my best
cold fingers pass over my eye (salt)
i flow under the beachball as green waves
which if it were vaves would contain
the picture (v) and the name (aves)
of knots : the beachball : the green sea
through the fireplaces spurting through the chimneys
the waves : the whales : the beachball on a seal
still : the green of days : the exit

ENTRY

major turnpike connections in eastern united states
audubon, witchcraft, akbar
all for san francisco

ordinary people
i have killed poetry
yes   and i had to tell you
books are dead
refer others to your own
experience perhaps
identical thoughts flicker
through each head at the same time
intelligence was the invader from space
and won   defend your planet

now that sounds intelligent

THE WHITE LADY

on the phone   meeting the white lady
smoke hangs solid in the cab   i speak to the driver
in spanish   the arrangements have been made

LIE STILL LIE STILL

o lady speak
for if there is a dream
then let it be
paranoia

is seeing how language works
what it means   the face of a wolf
glares back through the glass

blossom   honey
my favourite poem
is
still
is

MOONSHINE

the plastic back
of chairs – the

of chairs – the
look at that

my moment
what it should have

storm of static
with one line clear

TAXONOMY

the albatross drawer
this is the drawer where we keep the albatrosses

YOU CAN'T GET OUT

this is no way
to find me
you plot your own course

in the still dark room
the blue man's skin
shows white tattoos

and you read on
and but
and so slowly

BLUE PIG

hearing the paper hearing the sound of the pen
like a seance : i will dictate these words
who dat?   she had a woollen
hat : he was so *frien*dly then

?

animals of the north
my child is dead
therefore you do not exist

wind darkens picture grey to black
in the name of the father the son
and the holy spiral

a picture of the flatness it felt
sounds from another room
only the eyes move

ears cannot find the present
coupled onto the future
i can do nothing can the rain?

REFERENCE

this is the poem from which i quote
'this is the poem from which i quote'

SUNDAY DRAUGHT

studying zymology, and in particular zymurgy
watching the zymogenesis of the zymogens
counting the zygospores and zygotes after zygosis

zymosis! quick, the zymometer!

ON MY HOLIDAYS

i was born in the house of a rocket maker: the green stone
hand is for luck. all my teeth have been corrected – a small
thing in the life of a star, but who knows...? i like the
mountains, deserts, the sea and clouds. my ambition is to be
a magnet.

TRIBAL GOD

talk talk and then there is no-one, not even a telephone:
remains of eyebrows and detritus of the people and their
work. i am a speedy human and the noisy night air is so
filled with their dreams i am afraid to sleep. come to me,
lady: make me a perfectly wrapped chocolate bar. another
night with ruthless in my pocket.

NOT A STEP DO I STIR UNTIL THAT CAT'S BACK TO ITS COLOUR

civilization was pushing around aging molecules saying
"lovely...a new patch of lung" and "aching doesn't thank"
when a sunbeam hit my son, throwing his tiny full colour
    reflection
onto the centre of the flickering black and white screen

THE BECKONING HARPOON

my muse is bored with the company i keep. i wait for her to
flash the mirrored paper in my eyes and she does this.

UNIVERSITY DAYS

this poem has been removed for further study

CAP

pattern outside my head
speak to me
signaller of the word-commune

i was not aware
one lonely word outside
could call itself 'snap'

CANVAS

all blue
in the distance

i feel
i am

a
hologram

of static
in your life

PESSIMIST

little life supports my body
i don't want to be pretentious
this is the floor plan: here
is the hotel   i do my best

BREEDING THE ARSENIC-PROOF BABY

i see china as terribly peaceful   folk
sitting around saying "torch-singer roxy's
on the wire"   writing poems like

        "24 RIBS

pop   out flies the spirit"

i like to listen late at night
breathing in a tiny cloud of chinese skin
as they all jump up and down whispering "china"

OLIVE MANDATE

good luck jim olive mandate
takes top prize for every thing olive mandate
that the interest is changing forms olive mandate
these glasses are sensitive to infra red olive mandate
and i'm to be the old love he ran away with olive mandate

NORTHWEST OHIO

torn off
before toledo
and drowned at sea

the news appeared
accidently
as a message

TRACKING (notes)

light (drugs as only altering positions of piles of chemicals).
light as feeling? i.e. pulse waves(what happens to things
moving away faster than the speed of light? does light die
out?). jesus, shakespeare, hitler, etc. (political waves?) going
out from planet like heart beats.

light. dream being the mixed waves of feeling from other
'mind' sources during darkness – our consciousness(un is not
sub) due to nearness of *clear light source* (reflected light or
what? mirrors?). day – night: artificial light destroys balance
(midnight sun?).

☆

every question you ask presupposes
an alternative universe

☆

fibonacci numbers?
1:1:2:3:5:8:13:21:34:55:89 etc.

☆

saddle of *hare?*

☆

god is the space between thoughts, no, that's simplistic. some-
times you can't understand the words but you know the
medicine is right.

☆

for god's
sake
stay open
to your time

what's done
is

☆

train

    the night

        rain

☆

nothing

lasts

☆

within everyone is an antenna sensitive to the messages of
the time: art is beamed to these antennae. education should
tune them: instead they are smothered with phony 'learn-
ing'. the past has no messages (yes it has – whispering smith's
harmonica and a dog howling in the night).

☆

we

    are

        now

☆

not rejecting *knowledge* but what (as in research) passes for
knowledge and is but an illusion. the words (knowledge,
intelligent etc.) must be redefined, or new words coined.

☆

that is sure

   clear

☆

the connections (or connectives) no longer work – so how to
build the long poem everyone is straining for? (the synopsis
is enough for a quick mind now(result of film?) you can't
pad out the book)(a feature film with multiple branches:
you'd never know which version you were going to see).

☆

things of your time are influenced by the past. the artist can
only go on from there and use the situation *as it is:* anything
else is distortion.

☆

i stick with deKooning saying 'i influence the past' – and it is
not important for the work of a time to be available in the
mass media of its time: think of dickens on film, dostoevsky
on radio.

☆

the true direction is always a glancing off – there must be an
out – all truth is not *contained* in the language: it *builds* the
language.

☆

ahab: bringing back the light(whale oil?). darkness?

☆

who's done any work on moving of food from where it
grows? (connection to *land*).

☆

plane explosion – where do the sandwiches and suitcases land? killed by a flying gold tooth – is it treasure trove?

☆

white connected to *light* (link with white races fading?) the *concentrated* flashes of light from blacks' teeth/eyes?

☆

acid
or drink sweet drink
bananas and dates
disconnect battery

writing and i have a child
indigestion: fritz and su-su
          the intestine

sun leaves the leaves
send this and strawberry
chewing gum to aram

mara ot *mug* gniwehc
yrrebwarts *dna* siht dnes
sevael eht sevael nus

enitsetni eht
us-us dna ztirf: noitsegidni
dlihc a evah i *dna* gnitirw

yrettab tcennocsid
setad *dna* sananab
knird teews knird ro
dica

☆

92

into the side of the waterfall
    the depth of the image

☆

follow life
do not   despair
(the legendary cock-of-the-rock)
stay on the wheel
do not accept the illusions
i   sol   at   ion
of conservation and ecology
(or that's the way the llama breaks)

☆

the shadow and the sun vibrate
the circle and the shell

penumbra

dig///it

☆

the disguises
fit tight and are sealed

tasting to find what? spurt spurt
the positions of chemicals are altered

☆

the decision
is not provoked by flicker

so why does it articulate?

☆

what does the word truly mean?
how do we ask the question?

☆

beneath the tight bodice
a nipple lights
the investigation closes a door

☆

all week i've (week?) felt
the speed of writing
explanation rejects my advance

☆

models of the past

☆

agree to the movement
who are you?
your self faces you

☆

any   erg

anergy

☆

his neck was like pigskin
with the bristles still in

☆

laurent odour

☆

the curtains are closed
in the theatre
genetic reels
are stored in no time
and no space

but there is print through

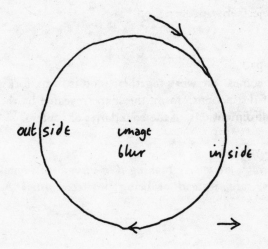

HOW TO PATRONISE A POEM

begin
welcome in

appear
poem
in these lines

i will
not draw
your picture

☆

no. the spark comes. we work together. oh it is form, form,
the making of distinctions. form, the shape revealed by the
detection, in all dimensions, of the boundaries of content.

☆

stunting their *own growth* ... making *themselves* ornamental
japanese trees, safe, instead of being the trees *struck by
lightning*.

☆

'extra yields
extra profits'

as if what they handle
were not alive

☆

life was the invader, perhaps, and all things that *live* were
members of the *crew* (animals went in two by two, yin and

yang) who survived through a warp into no-space between.

☆

i sense the end
down a tube
a spurt now and then

eighteenth to eighteenth
a choice
of the net's size and gauge

the ship is changing course
i have played out the games
and the old faces bore me

season to season
names flashing
i'll hammer it

so damn thin
i can see out

☆

our enquiry
points a way
off the wheel

eleven segments
are left to trust
and imagination

☆

lose
your   self

your   self
    becomes
your   art

then what is left

    lives

no matter how you muddy it

it clears
            and there you are

again

                                ☆

do you see me?
i am leaving a space
where i was   is as bad

                                ☆

i shall forge the blade
of my *own* substance

and it may not be a blade

                                ☆

i have tasted fire
goodbye, pleasant butter

AT MAXIMUM ZERO

seeking the still window
in stasis
a variant arrival
chortles into a hold-all
golden arrival-window

lo! nears the orgone-bug
– mincy ugly tunneler –
each distant foot feels all
eggy   agony in a homosexual's apartment
eggy future in a blimp sack

"ballast" (ricardo montalban)
a fat lip
leapfrogging
hold! ho! lobster's
name instructs the eggy cherub

WHAT DO YOU SAY?

low level plains and copses
a certain fierce time
hiding jokes in mud bricks
fierce coals and midnight embers

jerking a rabbit upwards
loving laughter and misty turtles
it is 1770 in reykjavik
singing   scheming   masking   killing

killing people with moderation
killing   never sinking a rock
seeing foam
taking a lovely levee

A MOST COLD

they hold isaak at fire
moulding the tundra
clear water and ice
a bold magyar
gorging

no merit gets oregon
mincing   ugly   vulgar
at leghorn fairs
each man takes with iron
isaak takes iron

iron blasts from calderon
a fiery kiss
hops
hold   o   languor
its name is lethe

WHAT YOU GOT?

the far-off cattle seem to clop
a steamboat to distend it
while day exacts a solid fee
the burning cattle mind it

but lo! a rabbit-cat appears
gambolling endearingly round and round
the seventeen zippers of its pelt
snag simultaneously on the ground

pets that have not learned moderation
whose energy forces them to roam
may end as half-chewed entrecôtes
beneath sweet turkish loam

FROM TIME TO TIME IN THE PAST

tree lets me hear the wind
over there where it is
i won't believe this is all there is
(the interest on eternity)

'it is' squeaks my voice

MIXED

whee! the tip of a lock
of her hair blows round
and round on the urban set
mocked up like your 'jungle'

but from deep in the tape
of tropical sounds
a good engineer brings out
first a splash in the surf

then 'we are lost' in her
father's voice: but ludwig's
ears were deadened
by the last of a species of bright birds

GASLIGHT

a line of faces borders the strangler's work
heavy european women
mist blows over dusty tropical plants
lit from beneath the leaves by a spotlight
mist in my mind a riffled deck

of cards or eccentrics
was i
a waterton animal my head
is not my own

poetry is neither swan nor owl
but worker, miner
digging each generation deeper
through the shit of its eaters
to the root – then up to the giant tomato

someone else's song is always behind us
as we wake from a dream trying to remember
step onto a thumbtack

two worlds : we write the skin
the surface tension that holds
                              you
                              in
what we write is ever   the past

curtain pulled back
a portrait behind it
is a room suddenly lit

looking out through the eyes
at a t.v. programme
of a monk sealed into a coffin

we close their eyes and ours
and still here the tune

moves on

NO + ON = NOON
(EXCEPT WHEN REFLECTED)

window stops at the edge of window and door at the edge of
the door: the observer shuts his eyes and continues the jour-
ney. memories eat away at the idea. wall runs into ceiling
runs into flex runs into bulb runs into light. already the
morning screams come from other rooms. dreadful as it
may be it is not so. dreams are sellotaped loosely on to the
ten pictures of 'loved by children' characters, all of whom
look the same way. chummily, their eyeballs roll towards
you. it splits like slate or mica: or a thin sheet of dream takes
the place of a feather in a golden oval. how to see people
without their clothes.

death comes because the power of the body to grow is finally
nullified by gravity (. . . 'seriousness'). to preserve itself, intel-
ligence must keep its captive, mind, far enough above the
surface to loosen the valves sufficiently for ideas to be pushed
into action. this is no time for padding or panic. nobody
controls the *dice* – when they roll the winner is he who pulls
the rest into the fork of his *number*. of course there is a path
where you never die, and a path where you are never born –
both, and all, are irrelevant (see "the blind deaf mutes' book
of dreams"). if at death your whole life passes before you
think your way out of that.

the letters come with thanks and any *fool* knows it's all
available: even for re-play, the repeated gesture. all those
napoleons like a deck of cards riffled though time. or that's
what his 'idea' would have you believe if you had time for
that. so the repeats go to the asylum because intelligence

can't have you reminded of *no-time*. think of the shock when the cameraman returns to collect his speeded-up film of a rose blooming and finds the flower has moved a yard to the east, out-of-focus. focus locus hocus pocus. if a whole science and language spring out of the word *mathematics* no, that's a trap. the notebook is always boringly open for our impressions.

SURGICAL NAMES : JOE

his head in silhouette is a dove
landed on his shoulders   the space
between hand, hip, his foot on her shoulder
is the shape of an hour glass   he will slip

this is a cracked caruso record
its effect on the world is yet to be discovered
◀———Eastern Airlines Route Map
(now that was a re-cap)

humidity affects all thoughts below cloud base
rain washes down fragments of ideas
to the waiting rats   who know
bts f th potry o kats, bake, an yats

yes, the sculpture is of a rat
rat-time rat time

to get back to the buffalo flight
zoo poem : (zoëtrope – look that up)
'the pen is mightier than the sward'
(an optical toy that shows
figures as if alive and in action)

SITUATIONS

inside
the pantomime horse

a door in the t.v. opened
i felt the draught

colonel
eternal

BOUNCE

the poor are painted out
the rich, powerful, and famous have their say

tomorrow will be everywhere
so why not call it today?

"hello tomorrow, this is
a wanderer among the voices"

some are pictorial
and even educational

try all the different bits

        fragmented

        sparkling

puff! i've put it out with my *hand*
and you all understand

LOVE AND PIECES

met language static
on the street
thinks he's one
of a new elite

☆

you have to learn
you can not teach

☆

"there goes the town of spanish boot"
"only the buildings"

☆

julius reuter
service de pigeons

☆

i can not prove a second ago
to my own satisfaction

WANDERING

terror of people leads into 'the people'
keep the message to your self
it's your journey

not to say the picture's wrong
but the hands
of the clock haven't moved

this has an archaic air like 'ere and o'er
make it fast
features formed by time's wind

dance inside the cloth
in a dull room
thin honey haze

this heavy haze
open the door
let it fight noise

lavender upon lime green
orange on dark brown
lost and am fishing

FUTURE MODELS MAY HAVE
INFRA-RED SENSORS

take a taxi and go fishing
how do you like that?
visit canada
hey look, i see a big moose

cat's nose is twitching
why don't you ever go
to work and earn money?
invest your money here

why don't you try it yourself?
i'm on guard duty
with the armoured car
could you give me a lift?

then we could buy some lunch
gentlemen, here comes lunch
there is all the food we want
just give me a microsecond

maybe you likee something
to eat while you wait?
of course, of course, well, well
i'll prove it to you

you sir. who, me sir?
well sir, what is the verdict?
believe me
i've never seen my sheet

tell me again, i don't get it
sorry, hotee dogs all gone
a natural using wild game
one share of wildcat oil

don't cut *me*. i never
heard of wildcat oil
broken glass, drawn stars
fine, fine, you killed him

hold it officer, it's my duty
right behind the car sir
before anyone sees me
my pleasure, you know what they say

money talks. i just don't understand
xylophone trills
another day like yesterday
we'll be in gravy

pardon me gentlemen
is there a bank
in the neighbourhood?
you drove up from hillcrest?

SONGS OF THE DEPRESSION

there's a shop on the road
we whiz by
slowing down from our speed
a turn off's an angle

talking the song through a kazoo
the giver of which
heads for switzerland
this thought holds it together

why four lines and a stapler?
why an address book?
a bottle of brandy? why
a key ring? an ashtray?

will you sit in the sun
or write a letter urgently?
how long will the candle melt
while i listen to the band?

grab it all and don't slow down
never leave the road for what's
in a shop or a store
the road's enough

why exclamation mark four
lines and a stapler glue
kleenex an envelope
shards of god

this is my table today
this is the sound
this is the noise through
my eye that spins around

PATCH PATCH PATCH

some evenings i think
of honour, glory, and bells

the last challenge is unanswered

cold night by the docks
captain bulb salutes another bottle

don't worry about that

in one part of the ship a phone rings
a message from another part of the ship

doppler effect

i don't know
where i can go
and sing the national anthem

everyone arrives at the ship on time
the girl, the golden-hearted drunk

"fuck it, finger, this poem *leaks!*"

MIRROR MIRROR ON THE WHEEL

what is my frame?
dry hot handkerchief
pressed to my eyes

unreal
i am examining
my love for this child

who looks so like me
i am inside
his movements

now he drops my keys
and stares
at the tapedeck

"all your sea-sick sailors
they are rowing home"
we hear

time, i love you
you are the way
i see the same anew

THE CONSCIENCE OF A CONSERVATIVE

if you are
a true machine
the edge is time
the edge is fine

☆

what have i lost
who are you

in the shadow
carved of wood

in the river
on this boat

always working
cancer mind

☆

o
hand
make a circle

how
the wound
snaps shut

☆

insulation
sun within mirrors
isolation

☆

hands and feet
of my soul

broken
pulled nails

curled back
in time

☆

time takes
me further
from grace

i have
never felt
so tired

afraid
invention
leaves me

once more
in my space
i dream

☆

on the shore where they "established a constant" (two palms,
blue sea) lay a dirty white sock, a pair of blue and white
tennis shoes, my feet (left resting on right). sound of a tram
(at night) in my head. volume, tone, and distance.

☆

jerky people on the street
i have not thought myself

one of you for a long while

you wear colours and move
among them: how does the force pass?

cool breeze communication
with your thumbs in your pockets
cold night air   the voices all around

☆

harsh light i will write openly
too much
one way

☆

clothes
stationary through the night

☆

"a history
of ideas"

☆

we will live through
a long boring time
of everybody having "insights"

a little gold creeps in
an urge for distinction
description – it *mat*ters

☆

bleak

☆

compass rose

☆

a shadow / is something / on the surface
therefore
through our transversion of time
forgotten

☆

a babylonian rage : the car misses and aches

glow

☆

all this gets us nowhere
no there's no where   now here

☆

coughing
echo of metal from stone

the light
that lets
me read
and write

☆

seeing in a
"wrong light"

☆

life : half of all opposites in any direction

the opposite of "book"

the opposite of "high" is "pink"

☆

the letters said
we are here for a serious purpose

trial bores into time

☆

only the stone
smoke curling
film knows my hate

for the lamp
is open
the bulb unbroken

☆

boo

del

wah

☆

speak my language

dog

☆

in this ward
i can but draw

nameSeman
nameSeman

☆

imagine

being

and not

knowing

☆

my first is in move but never in door
my second's in emit but never in floor
my third is in time and also elastic
my fourth is in era and yes it's in plastic
my fifth is in wrapt and double in wrapped
my sixth is in home but never in mapped
my seventh's in or and also in open
my eighth is in or and never in open
my whole is a word whose meaning's unclear
is it this? that? or what? will it last? am i near?

☆

a turtle

a fine line

a turtle

☆

primitives

see

they eat
all the meat

☆

set

sorce

de

hote

kwolitay

☆

there's a star in my film
i keep trying to pick it out

☆

epateRetape

FUNERAL CARDS

if they do
what you think
it's as boring
as you thought

☆

"let's just say
you gave my imagination
full rein"

☆

i put it
there
and it's still
there

☆

round
and round
and round

☆

"the dead end kids
(here with bogart)
represented the depression's
displaced teenagers"

☆

i:
am
in the past

☆

orange
genius
experience

☆

moon to breathe

☆

small moon was not even part of the poster
when ants arrived to give all 'the solution'
if this train is a light   who are we?
where dot dot where dot dot where

☆

nothing
is not even
nothing wrung out with full strength

☆

an
acute
sense
of
old

☆

cut off
pictures
without
the dream

☆

lord
of night
staff of agonies

☆

there's safety
in numbers
ann finnegan
my cousin

☆

this

alien

language

☆

o.k.
captain

☆

in a
speed
boat

☆

clean
print

☆

no longer
any interest
on my life

☆

coloured
shadows
redefine

no more
i hope
there is

☆

continual

correction

☆

"say hello to your people"

PERPETUAL MOTION

tanks
go into
battle

☆

the arabs photograph themselves
from the israeli point of view

☆

looking back
looking forward

☆

through
eating
biting
chewing
up to ten whole hours

☆

for people
who don't like
the real thing

☆

cleverer
speaking
honestly

☆

small shipments of white arms

☆

some think it's to do with the line

☆

no thank you
i don't play with watches

☆

effective
november first

☆

take it
and bake it
and wrap it
in under

☆

the myth
of creation

☆

now

then

charlie

☆

exposes
them
to extreme danger

☆

learning to see what others see
there is no superiority

☆

complete with everything you see

☆

mission impossible tape reading

☆

admit to bean

☆

reception

☆

je ne veux pas
les biscuits chocolats

☆

warp

lanes

☆

a cat's concept of the mind
that could make it dance
and sing by editing film

☆

mary
was assumed
into heaven

☆

slowly
through the

snow they
go

☆

open
pour
and
store

☆

what ever
you heard

☆

love in mind

sun through the blind

☆

splendid

olig

☆

crime the adrenal
time the pineal

☆

far away
a pie
in the high
sierras

☆

on trick plays
he'll use his

head, nose, eyes, face

☆

with power
speeding power
slowing no
emergency

☆

attached
to
awards
power

☆

home   work

☆

met

his

match

HORSE POWER

interchange of display
arrival of the colonel
aquatint

no way

intelligent echoes in colour

but i

can't

help

falling in love

with

you

☆

slavery

what

we

have

words

for

☆

always looking through the eyes
he only knows the sausage is after him

☆

remember
no time
when i wasn't

☆

"you're a honky-tonk
i'm a record-player
playing a honky-tonk"

☆

captain terminal

☆

"in which we have made
enormous progrom... *progress*"

☆

the puzzled house awaits my tail
1600 pounds of nervous elephant
you are watching   lavinia

stolen or invented but proffered
boredom   red-hot thumbs
light passes through the crest

the narrative continues trapped
i enter listening watching waiting
ing ing ing   a mis-spell   ing

☆

what:
a form

☆

no-one

will ever
find out

☆

sustain this to the ear-ring
french windows blown open
flames of three lamps

carrying an extinguished candle
no, alight: the swinging cut glass
of the candlestick   murder   commercial

☆

the blot leading the knot

☆

in notification for this case
we have extracted our peripheral business
everyone was the aim but then
anyone woke up

brain reacts to fear
curved into its present form
o i'm lazy
bored or tired

☆

needs

open up the gallery

no space

☆

"peace and value, comrade"

☆

"run a loss on him"

☆

on top
of the lift

☆

starts to work instantly

☆

i met my fate but the seams didn't match
bulbs spelled l o a n s
fat of the famous touched in mime

☆

no longer addresses
how can we know
the first
goodbye

☆

too late
what rhymes with cow
and starts with an n

☆

black holes in the metaphor

lost my sense of fun
found it had met death
observed it with pauses
was lonely and attached

all hands on time observe
the symbols   wearing away
a woman singing   new york
thank you distracters

her slowness extends not out but in
she licks her plate
lamps instantly chosen music
death in a pattern by diamond

try to not feel interference
mein mind has nozzink to do
when i think blue
that is all i have to do

                ☆

unlock
tassel
painting
recorder

harmonica
message
friendship
border

seal
golden
weeks
american

yesterday
behalf
return
regard

tiger
way
compelled
communist

get
returned
should
disavow

☆

like

so and so

unknown

unknown

☆

para   sol

☆

use
of a cat

power
of money

value
of life

CODA: SONGS OF THE MASK

mad
she said she'd personally see i lost every patient i had

☆

you don't know what it means to be one-sided
you can always see both points of view
how very very very very very
very very very boring for you

☆

mimicked him so exactly
are
tha

all i'm going to
not
do

☆

can there be less
over there what're
a conscientious objector you
town and he knows

☆

maybe running out of time
time is frozen light
light

From ACE

in think

new face
from my home
what do you think
i'll voice out
of the news
alive and in love
drill
another hole
near the edge
of the label and
play it
from there
with a light
pickup
bless you brother
yours
till the energy
gaps again
let light
blink
history think
leaves some thing
like a bomb
relief again
to sail
against depression
i glow

and flicker
change
but first
a present
that
fits me
to a t
no mist
but sky
and we
beneath it
in our minds
never
prevented
life growing
by caring
we changed
selfishness flashes
SHOCK
SHOCK
in the mountains
we
used
SHOCK
SHOCK
feel through
that pack
aging
i will
not break
into
where at least

now
SHOCK
SHOCK
spare change
will
thinking light
hand
nothing
on
painted light
"i am into" or
"absorbing"
follow
the rebel
with
your eyes
sucking
the sky
of dust
leaves
untouched
as the wind
mixes us
with each breath
loose energy says
fill me
still
energy
hovers
(molecules
have manners)
tubed thought

is out to lunch
what pond?
are we at lake?
or a life
at sea
let me be
from proportion
out of
date
has its bad side
drifted a
way you see
that penicillin flush
she's on
winning
by verbal grace
beneath arches
no
mad
awakes
we do not feel
strangeness
he wakes
in terror
from a dream
different
eyes
want nothing
how easily
he is adviced
alive
each day

repeated
he lives
for ever
he thinks
alone
in the honey
comb o
the subjunctive
that riffle
of the deck
wind
here the surf
hits the beach
drum
pit
we're
through
the view
changes
tone
he dreams
his father
dead "no
my father
is alive
and in
'heaven'"
parentheses
more space
for a
while
he breathes

he does
not mean
you cannot
be he
too late
for the telling
harm
less
no
mad
less
a head he sees
their friends
their world
stain
between
sheets
of glass
eye
in the sky
then moon
now he
cannot
see
he
she
or it
water foams
cross him
just
going
wind blows

sand
and
him into
his traces
pick it
at the rat class
on enormous
ideas how
far
in hail
later
he visits
a fine
passage
where
the action
is
surrounds
itself same
thoughts
fewer
barriers
wander
who leads
leaders
any thing
but
himself is
strange
back
in the fold
he is in

a position
to recommend
his name
change
piece
precious
to think
down the beach
a fire
cold
moon
wants space
beautiful
in shadow
no first
no
second
meeting
how
i hear it
now
waves
all you
can do
with power
a thing
has no
intention
unknown
draws me
to him
alone

at
the waves edge
for now
a lawn
of pronunciation
in
a suburban
back
garden
smells sweetly
in warm air
pushes
him out
as no
mad
smile
feeling
uppermost
in his mind
puts wind
to back
as light
ups
sail
for life
laughs
to sky
original
out
standing
art in
junction

expounds
only
one
love
is well
we are here
before the standard
planes
corruption
chemical
change
a river
heads
in
land
place she
is different
the home
service
the light
programme
the third programme
she has
his message
reflect
atoms
gather
within
his nose
they eat
together
SHOCK

SHOCK
around them
words
clutter
me
me
face enters
not me
use
no
mad
for feeling
me
and
it
is a song
cloud
white
night
moon
o tell
imagine
if you
were how
would
you feel
ERASE
ERASE
repair
alter
their raft
sky

returns
no image
all
but strongest
poison
virus
flowers effect
but they
are in
drive
and
floating
my tongue
ear
gives warning
vowels
by light
bits
corner
marks
moon
in cancer
to go
beside
changing
lights
seldom
to want
peace
my ancient
bones
his feet

banner
toes
correction
spread
before
this train
approves
blue
strengthens
green
diminishes
red
slow
as it
seems
why
not
a little
difference
each
time
certain
gambles
she grows
dark
tonight
you
will represent
me
river
forks
round island

we think they
i don't get
the
connection
you will
you would
accept
a director
who left
it
to you
what can
they have
but beauty
for that
contest
no
mad
has seen
the island
ends
he
she
it
i
i
i
trinity
wins
by length
he said
this line

has no beginning
no
end
for furniture
that
doesn't
breathe
creation
recognition
how many
he sees
a
cross
connection
well
it will
keep you
off the
streets
under
standing
flowers
with kindness
you know
makes the drain
and the drano
end
of fantasy
make them see
that bore
old
emotions

body
wants
to go on
mekon
on
my mind
she is
my closest
friend
sun
shines
does not
every thing
blind
sail
through
no light
i talk
to my
self
assume
no
compulsion
at best
communication
brain   damage
mind
matter
what
an apple
why
a clutch

who
motion
where
mind
and i
spy
within
for pattern
together
they smile
at the stone
FADE
FADE
up
choosing
lunar
land
horses
don't move
wrong
and on
lost
consonants
speed
see clearly
nomad
your name
nothing
new
see
as far as
yucatan

momma
truth
there
is no truth
recoil
murmurs
notational
creational
rock
baby
sleeps
scarlet
light
snares
pause
to
slow
movie
halves
nice people
they turned
me in
SPACE
SPACE
exhale
talking
music
perches
mad
fascinating
mad
retreat

in
to
dream
just
makes a
pattern
no
mad on
grass
breathing
returns to his
senses
surf
to land
again
BOUNCE
BOUNCE
or just
continue
while
moments
wait
self
forged self
repairing
dreams
widely
sahara
entire
groups
but list
who comes

beside
life
strange
friends
change
was
coldest
not
miserable
worship
mad
no
mad
lost
treachery
led to
shaking
hands ·
will
you use
it
regularly
dream
by which
we see
at night
westward
leading
strength flows
in warm shadows
how many
of these

were made
inland
trees
cluster
sun
on water
filtered
screen
print
too slow
film
so much
perfection
this shore
of stone
remains
do not mock
those who died
in luminescence
or in pride
we stand
on memory
at war
white moves
into mind
FLASH
FLASH

in mind

nothing
behind poetry
look
a
like
or is it
an an
but
why
so
there
fore
because
maybe
if now
might
well
for it
let
go
un
hand
me
my good man
i'm a
gone
thank
god
norman
and henry bones

the boy
detectives
joipes!
rather
a line
from my left eye
to
the
tree
FLASH
FLESH
eye
o you
see
an
allegory
on the phones
to a shan't
same
place
does not
break the
thread
audition
(joke called it
brown)
all
senses
gone
could go
on
for ever

records
of shock
spin a
cross
eternal
thought
you'd go
that way
was aced
by payment
let's
leave
this zoo
clear
as a picture
some
times
painted
act
or object
erase
art
of the past
no longer
in terms
of size
STUCK
STUCK
to be
accepted
for the apple
in the picture

mister raworth
continues
to believe
every
thing
possible
no true
story
friend
to any
word
phew!
here's the
weather
forecast
for to
night chicawgo
and area
mohawk four
four one hundred
all that english
effect
so to speak
you know
who the star
is
softens into
a ring
takes place
here
added a
near enough

each time
a total
rip through
scans
fashionable
for that
west
wind
laughing
modality
of egg
plant
takes
place
so far
within
zero
in fall
flash
trap
plastic
wrap
use your
oven
more
to
two
too
ACTION
ACTION
figure
moves

jerkily
through silver
crystal
snaps
at the edge
of sound
contact
as
contract
free
ergs
reduce our
empire
adrift
in all senses
but one
stash
full of
armed
dope heads
power
cancer of
help
preserve
the lone
ranger
to be
solace
shapes
through adjectives
mist
opens

idealists
believe
clear
thinking
dialogue
dates
what said
call it
brain
nothing
but many
names
boredom
always
central
will
be
idea
technique
lingering
on every trait
out of focus
certain
territory
for fire
fattens
that's mohawk four
four one hundred
coming
through
splashed
wall

paper
good as
gun
SHOT
SHOT
under
SPOT
SPOT
light
a clue
to what
home
first
slakes
whistle
for fear
stays
in air
forever
magnifies
concentration
for
silver shines
mis
fortune
reappears
clad
as fog
simpers
fear
fully
glad

fright
fully
extended
syntax
considers
gold
power
squeaks
trivia
as echoes
through
yes
one strawberry
arcane
please
pour
in powder
tradition
of apple
scent
through no
other
eyes
no
communication
furnace
sings
love
now
if you
will turn
slowly

in sun light
cast
a way sentences
hold our
breath
shadows he
becoming
she (dat's
da *ser*pent)
imprints
for the master
tape
by the way
this is not
eastern
flames
natural
within
sophistication
creatures
of power
suck
authority
springs during
concentration
new face
from my home
with no thing
but english
face
air
with fish paste

tapes
an era's
music
TIME
TIME
admits
pidgin
moult
indifferently adverbs
pass degree
as nomad
meets ace
thought
in marble
soothed
by hands
no metal
makers
of job
hope you
do your
best under
any circumstances
sound
the tune
of the time
this
is not
the me
that felt
memory
all

that links us
elaborations
of the servant
class
put your
thinking caps
on
opposite
threat is
bribe
to let mood
move
with all haste
to appreciate
champions
watch
in slow motion
remember
and imagine
spin
to reflect
us
at night
weight
of light
lifted
pictures
any pattern
show me
what you
SEE
SEE

light
relief
in
da alley
lookat
good
will
be found
address
yet
proud
to be
a
winner
baby
sighs
just
the pattern
you see
with a lot less
trouble thanks
to you
supremes
and rolling
stones
always
nothing
left
to copy
canal theory
ace
i see

in all
i am
not here
may you
have
a small
foundation
when the winds
of changes
shift
if that's
what reality is
a glowing face
that seems to know
please
on dirt
piero
too
had that idea
voices
decay
into time
of what
is it
memory
writing
pattern
spelled
change
unreel
twist
tone

i am
again
wait
ace
faithful to
ace
flash
sears
what ever
is not
no
madness
does not
watch
the movie
science
of
detection
using
computers
for random
no
longer
motion
less

THAT MORE SIMPLE NATURAL
TIME TONE DISTORTION

slow
low
thump
long flame
dry
flash blur
just
move
tree browns
to south
our horse
white
no trace
of action
in memory
and fear
but this
is
clear
this area
this never
ending
song
to last
gasp
cold colours
enough
flashes

to leach him
out
as she
sparkles
that i will bear
two faces
and allegiance
mister cheap justice
bubbles
in
the silent
night
no control
over
extremities
bark
companion
words
twist off
what has
no name
salt
dragon
cartoon
cactus
close up
to empty
face
or back
of head
he could
be going

any
way
the presence
of nothing
slow
remember
food
this one
is still
grey
sound
stripes
layer
swift
so seal
of approval
leaves
no impression
see
possession
know
whimper
warm red
looks
at me
real
just went
by
late
again
slash
lights

diagonal
direction
of icy
moon
howl
scratch
soft knuckles
at the door
above
the tempo
flesh
tuner
shriek
right
we slide
out
into
filtered
footstep
mimic
ape
read
new
solids
not
pressed
prayer
aware
my brothers
we
for the love of
god

enter
spaces
of tradition
lean
far star
seen
atween
car
jar
keen
ears ending
tone
spheres
contending
alone
i love
empty
books
don't you
so
my awakened
spirit
weeps
i
can imagine
not imagining
that
STARTS
you
stay here
fall
in love

meet
mister
metaphor
shoot it
from cold
words
used out
give
space
TREMOR
TREMOR
stillness
of
my present
moves
within
me
chill sheets
chime
stained
ice
shatter
shadows out
without
falls
in
to memory
edmund
dante
caught
by a thought
nature

inclines
towards
risk
no
further
than you
can go
tempo
moon
my tube
moon
slow behind
silence
peace
or play the
game
i love
your music
muse
nor will
silence
slide
those fibres
of my love
for vanity
disfigures me
why cold
if ay
reflection
flames
to memory
games memory

of games
then silence
wakes me
with a
break
in waves

EURODE

sometimes the subtle night of sleep bores
music remembered places followed to despair
façades no substance aids my mood
i walk more clumsily
plane falls
in flames
o possible beauty   o lady
to trust without power
no end to reach
sun throws smoke shadows brown
acróss the page
my father was in burma during the war
it's easy to outsmart me
old sadness and the pain returns
drives light unowned and sound
of other off
my night ahead
remains
maybe the streetlamp's shine
will light the ending of this line

dead red of midnight
silent plants
changed shadows on the wall
now moon i feel you mould my pain
stay in your motion   grate against this bone
re
mind me
how once we danced around the table
o cancer   live plastic
down two tenths of a point

you played me on the screen
in a dream   speedy mind
sometimes i tire and live in memory
clear frames of love
burn off the shiny seals of fact
lead me in silence to the simple task
of easing through each day
who works not for us all is dumb
image blind
doubt crossed my mind

PRETENSE

a shiny black coffin inlaid with silver diamonds. face more perfect than life. simple problems. removing the area of revulsion (for want of a better word). capsules of air beneath the city: around them cartoon cats' eyes blink in the dark: above them molecules flash back to their past. we can make them smaller, too – or personalise the shape of a lapel. bugs playing with boys. personality static deforms tree rings: building a new road but free will holds us into pattern. such a time to climb out of the gene pool i'm not going back, copper! star fire.

it's dark as a dungeon down deep in the mayan: blurred ink looking for a good restaurant: 'sea level'. hunters with un-listed numbers sift for licenced movement as a consequence of the abundance of the plot – truth in the wrong accent. ladies and gentlemen, in this corner: the market. the fight: to preserve greed. image as two beige flat cardboard boxers fades away (out) (off). three gunmen with eight hostages flash up respect for the other's intelligence. "go on...tell us." "no...it's a secret." cope, chasuble, float to the ground. spin. put the bird in the cage.

i declare unequivocally that the centre of australia is whatever the abos project: cute lil things. it would improve our intelligence if we cut back on size. "simple to say" curt slurred, putting down the newspaper. yes...the centre of australia: where the hole is in the doughnut: where a holographic statue of peter finch crucified shares space with the thought of a duck-billed platypus. a sharp breeze lifted the ink from a front page picture, and between the dots, as it flapped off, sunlight charred a white shadow (after fifty-nine and a half) at the pole.

see how you can saw with a pioneer on an apparent plateau the heart's two-in-one collar. sharply split members loggedup, ready for more deterioration. broken near bottom and top, too rich for some pallids, they banjoed the monroe doctrine right near the fan. weather manipulation graduates specialised apart: some became their fields: some still looked like their pets. light burn tracks led curt to the easter island wigstands. his mirage map was torn. grey blurs in the fibres made, as they met, a chinese subtitle of their usual stiffness. it's time to introduce sally nighter.

double-acre handouts, dream flames, possible loops without leaving the ground, stertorous breathing, lumps in the bishops' benevolence: all these in a trunk sprayed angularly blue through rivet holes. a male intercept programme of its own. pore city. sally had trouble with her vowels: any sound in that framework echoed through the handspread. no questions asked. certain separations of all colours were her steps around the spiral of abbreviations. understandable segments clicked references into deep grooves filled with luminous paint. she had no dares: nor did the limits of light scour her imagination's black felt. she regularly ate her hearing.

she certainly did – and while curt was in alaska. but, on a day when no surprise could interest, watch him slowly duck, padding out his upper lip with polar bear hairs. in absolute silence an anonymous citizen is tep'd out. curt graduated in waking. his face is drawn in charcoal without believing it. he collects old news and can always find something to focus on. india clicks in behind him and he touches its smooth cold with his nose. inspired by fact, sally waves to him. they switch out of gear as planets are rinsed and hung to dry.

kill in the dark light, by lines, mamma mia: in accents that depend for their force on glass transmission. any symbol in uniform can construct a complaint. disparity slid between its meaning. draughts. curt's shower of sparks? – "feel ease you crane!" sally was there, seeing dignity in dark and plump meat. driving across country the annual state of onions was obvious, even to a plastic pipe. fanlights gave that little extra. he couldn't even read: everything had failed – except motion. sally had a sense that any transfer meant the total degradation of style (which she saw as permanent change).

spiral anything through and you'd catch them both on the porch. mosquitoes couldn't see yellow, but crackled on their way to black light. immediate sounds dispersed. alone, his fantasies left everything as it was. a huge revolving magnetic disc shortcut the "hello, i'm blank" label. based on rigidity, believable colour flooded the steaks as steamed letters told him what he was. sally still liked the tingle of snow anytime the actual could be blanked out. join us for all the news an hour from now if texas don't melt with all that ice-cream. no memories keep them in the landscape.

fine tuning spat out another engraving, waxing and waning in a torrent of whorls. souls: they too have souls. bank imperial almost proved you could get your own money, at least. three physicists headed for white-on-white could almost stay half-awake for half-an-hour (during which they weren't quite themselves, but types of 'high priest' – a convenient way of breakfasting in bed). day wuz all running down da barber's pole, as it revolved, almost cornering what they thought of (when half-asleep) as tiny black holes. curt put his hat over their square pegs in an act of heresy.

safety crews are on hand immediately to attempt extrication of the driver but he exits alive from the holocaust. they kiss under her hat by the blind computer remembering all those "stop press"s anamorphically smeared on the news star or standard. slowly pink stains the mist. when the great anagram is written, and the hordes of symbols and examples swell into the dimension of truth, clouds may still drift from the centre. turning and twisting through the various growth (or age) stages of vineyards and apple orchards, the road led to the outskirts of town, where many selves waited for the next cheap fix.

solar waking, trunks warming, blue jays machine-gunning those parachutists in red or blue overalls we see, from the battlements, climbing the hill. following the printed instructions curt made a paper gasmask ("fold over and back to flag"), but when he clamped it over his nose and mouth his ears rang with deafening pressure. he had been allowed just enough time to do everything. the variety of his notations flickered from coyote howls to the proposed police department submarine. sucking dream from the shudder of balancing the morning, he sealed that little hole in the fabric with clear tape.

stream traceries of shifted cloth patterned after some ritual. spanish shawl of love and affection: y'all heah dat break? look you, my breathers and system – if you can't handle what's put in, who are we? pay for their arming with taxes while you're charged with hardening a fugitive. one of them was a fine-talking lemon (the bank was non-equipped with any surveillance cameras). in a minute house a mile from the capital building this has been those. hey! don't squeeze through reverbs, honey: your life is of random worth to those nervous survivors "on the hill".

you'll feel it get bigger and bigger as it gets wetter (shrug): a yellow overshift in a memory not projected on the optic nerve. sound fuzzed by a loose diaphragm, curt put down the comb and watched the paper float to the floor. rosa had subdued her metamorphosis as he repeated the question "who chose the logo?" a puff of dust took the glare from his hair. he had a lot of graphs, arrows...things like that. uh ...throwing out the set of appliances with the bathwater as the woman said. a tidy living.

the simple properties of anthem – advocated by the doctor of arabic – squirreled up the trunk and stovepipe of her haid. sally believed nothing of this with her two eyes: nothing drew nearer: now nothing is further from the truth, fonder glass. those rills and torrents, those spumed peaks, those kangaroo courts, those réalités (pardonnez-moi). curt saw hawks pecking, a dog roll over and leave bearing two children, an old man (his cane graduated in inches) waving dots in grey. educated by climax.

sometimes cellbursts bubbled pictures in curt as he re-condi-
tioned. everchanging faces constantly recognisable swam,
poised, and moved off-screen. they stopped at a synthesis-
bar for a wavelength-stripe. sally subbed a reflex laugh into
the station jam. meanwhile "if that is in me, who's looking
at it?" – mister thryce had hidden behind a newspaper until
now. with a muted "roast BI-ssimo" he farm-talked his way
through the hyphens: "too many news" his final bubble. this
one in circumstance of colour swung his name. "collections
...start your collections!"

north america is europe meeting africa and south america:
but that doughnut will still twist asia – transistor heirs gib-
bering over raw kangaroo. blink. blink. blink. they go off in
zoos worldwide. briefly maps reveal (as a magnet flashes
iron filings) another shape. aber herr thryce is waiting for
the verb. "australise?" sally queries. bad imprints as in a
flush new blood washes the brain of curt's theory clear of
mis-representation. a refined taste, more local than a speedy
anaesthetic. waiting for the ninth mode in a flip freeze. tell
you what, she'll sing it in italian.

GRACIOUS LIVING 'TARA'

lonely as four cherries on a tree
at night, new moon, wet roads
a moth or a snowflake
whipping past glass

lonely as the red noses of four clowns
thrust up through snow
their shine four whitened panes
drawn from imagined memory

lonely as no other lives
touching to recorded water
all objects stare
their memories aware

lonely as pain
recoiling from itself
imagining the cherries
and roses reaching out

MAGNETIC WATER

glare burns of nothing very near in time
surfaces split and go their own ways
in the breeze of light   so too this image
lengthens nothing   i praise your light
against the night whose skin
glistens with moving cloudy white

those burns were of themselves the image
as was the breeze   one surface was of film
the character half drawn   one coloured
the night air bright with nothing but reflection

then from my death i felt that all must die
that holding in our time was black
and cold   that rocks glowed red
that trees which formerly i climbed
swayed from their roots
in one direction   i heard
me fumbling through the scores
of ancient scripts
as forces struggled for my arm
while thought as muscle lifted from the pool
a silent waterspout whose touch
sucked out one convolution of my brain

the letters danced with changing shape
one two three four   all sound poured in
those several openings of the tube
flexed   doors on the air   no floors

empty we think we know what comes
lip readers of the slowed heart's valve
don't hear the music of those crystals set
in joints of syntax cry
love is our salve
believe us or we die

A SILVER BULLET MADE FROM A CRUCIFIX

forgotten
heads of gold sparks
loom in the night

you have the right to do anything
by agreement
you see they're burning this afternoon

stake my heart
no awareness overlooked
is called the addend

forgotten
heads of gold sparks
shine in the night

EVERYTHING I HAVE IS YOURS

yes i believe you always are
though clutter of life divert me
everywhere a mind may wander
you wait for space to clear

your little hat is made of time
you turn your nose up at a rhyme
you make me laugh with beauty
which is joy, nay, i say

those ships down there to your right
in the coloured bit
are waiting for you to bend and peel them off

LENIN'S MINUTEMEN

a grain of terror
a fifty dollar painting
we were detained by chaos
i was just asking

flash back to the ceremony
a welter of pretend
some got a lot of money
unrelated to value

heard voice saves work
mister clipper
i hope you forgive me
for not believing the rational map

true : see the great serpentine
wall : your energy has gone
no time for turnips that
would be discriminatory

fragment 66 diogenes of oenoanda
proposition 31 spinoza (concerning god)
fool's gold
a biography of john sutter

i shall return home
to find my heart
in the honesty of man
far outacite

PRATHEORYCTICE

as i think of rolling up the dogends
looking for papers
i see this terrible thing
thought of as a better life
sometimes i wonder
what is introspection
red white and blue
or through mud and blood
to the green fields beyond
which were the colours on a tie

ROME BY ANONYMOUS

mirrors show only her changing lips
discount is discussed behind shelves
another smile: messieurs mesdames
eyelashes half a block long

dusty gloss pulls right
another bus with faces looking
walking delicately on her heels
stranger leaves

anyone could show the emperor blue
but the order goes to the assistant chef
two olives, salad in styrofoam
anyone to wipe his fingers on

not traced by us is the only book that really belongs to us. not that the truth, they are arbitrarily chosen. the books whose hieroglyphs are patterns formed by the pure intelligence have no more than a logical, a possible upon us, it remains behind as the token of its necessary truth. the ideas printed in us by reality itself. when an idea – an idea of any kind – is let in dictated to us by reality, the only one of which the 'impression' has been laborious to decipher than any other, is also the only one which has been the most austere school of life, the true last judgement. this book, more listen to his instinct, and it is this that makes art the most real of all in art and intentions count for nothing: at every moment the artist has to intellect supplies us with pretexts for evading it. but excuses have no place genius, that is to say 'instinct'. for instinct dictates our duty and the these are mere excuses, the truth being that he has not or no longer has the moral unity of the nation, he has no time to think of literature. but this book: he wants to ensure the triumph of justice, he wants to restore war, furnishes the writer with a fresh excuse for not attempting to decipher to evade this task! every public event, be it the dreyfus affair, be it the aside from writing! what tasks do men not take upon themselves in order our work for us or even collaborate with us. how many for this reason turn any rules, for to read them was an act of creation in which no-one can do exploring the ocean bed), if i tried to read them no-one could help me with

SLEEP, PERCH

each clearing of the brain
needs nothing to be clear again

i don't want to listen to the same
i don't get it better twice

starve the nation
out of stagnation

wandering the earth
a civil war ahead of the traffic

MORDANT FLEAS

today it is raining in geometry
x-ray pulses brake soft rock
utah   top right chinese mind
echo within   matter collapse
in flatland, sweet flatty flatland

the urgent view is recognised
ninety-eight dollars a year
flies it in   signed
adolph s. ochs, publisher
acadian, donc

they are suckers they don
the plant as a watch
whose time is same emotions
reappearing beneath the sun
they think in a lineup

well i think a war is
kind of special a little
out side that's mine
o coin de la rue
o gold wash through

From WRITING

spears of laughter
hiss for a time
then clank across
leaving flakes of rust
to fox pages
as the sepia picture
goes full colour
and begins to move
but for now
we get the idea
birds' eye view
see the words try
to explain what
is going in there
an imagined book
coming in to focus
the scene
in which the book rests
is stationary
only
within the moving picture
is anything happening
sound
for the moment
is not memorable
so we drive off
in any distraction
for example
how long
i can hold
my interest

may be
a silken thread
part of the binding
useful
to mark where
to go back
whence
to continue
blue and red
embossed rocks
line upper right
lower left
certainly
today was windy
a fifty thousand
diploma
should be worth
a future
please wait
till you exit the system
to resume eating
plays on
under ground steam
frozen
as earth
blurs our picture
your country gives you
metal pieces
coloured
by fragility of life
a belt buckle
of imitation antique brass
flickers in as
though the cuts

were frame to frame
while memory nags
at persistence of vision
from screen to drawing
no matter
what
is a sudden change
for in this area
that cannot be
called a landscape
as anything may happen
i turn to write
instead of read
waking this morning
with a sore head
fading memories
of dream advice and image
aram without shoes
a display on poland
black and red
holes in the framework
back stairs smaller
rooms leading into others
posted results
of random examinations
always foretold
by intensity of teaching
so five white flowers
stand out against
the blind turned dark
by the reflection
of the rising sun
and brighter still
the building now revealed

by drifting fabric
balances a slice
of clear sky cut
by three black cables
by the frame
our object glimmers back
we imagine at
page one the title

"CREDULITY"

as our glance
follows the wires
downhill
in white shoes
a chinese drunk
sights an umbrella
at their swaying
shadows on his wall
genes change
through clear memories
of similarity
as our propellor
whirs off the spiral
a poem

"REFORMED CHURCH

my company was
founded on dirty money"

ocean
of oil
bubbles on water
on the border
of the new we
cannot look behind
us sheltering
in our shadows
stumble those
who will not look
themselves
within theirselves
dark holds no absence
i am why you
who ever must
be also here
watching the frame drop
onto an actor's head
over words telling
where we are
silently
the book glows
silver   red   blue
the text begins

"BEYOND ME

they're not real
this is real
captain blood
how image attracts
through time
vanity
a parrot on my shoulder

not the sameness
of sun
but a grey winter evening
a trace of rain
wind rising
snow light
slowly
this clears
pleasure from words
pleasure from shaping the letters
easing my spine
however i wish
revolving my head
to a strychnine arc
strangers in my dreams
quite adroit
not too hilarious
children
dance to static
in the kitchen
the idea
is suffused with light
a suffusion
of light
not memory
but once only
way not only
form
but manner
still
i gave the matter
some thought
off into sound
red pointing fists
float

to real blood
we
flash back
on is present"

how you would play
with that
idea my friend
as through the texture warps
a previous song called

"HAPPY BIRTHDAY BING

clarity of another mind
spinning so i see through
too, to a view
of rearrangements

i could set back
this against black
it glows   he knows

light has been caught
and as i explain
i want to feel this pain

no longer
die, nerves, burn out
release me   how my shout
drifts through that whirring mind"

lies
lies
pictured as a bent photograph
etched

on a two way mirror
eggshell
endless words
how i see
is alien
you sing a little
then i sing a little
every time
we say goodbye
what do you battle
for
to be best
you
as a better me
i agree
to show you what i see
egg   moon   acquent   apolune
pivot
on the front step with

"FAMILIAR QUOTATIONS

asleep
by thy murmuring stream
falls, with heartache
each in world of his own
asleep
hope they have not been
in lap of legends old
keep it quiet till it falls
devil is
lips of those that are
man
time has fallen
tide as moving seems

never see ticket unless
the very houses seem
who knows not that he knows is
awake
my soul
my st. john
arise or be forever fallen
men, are in one common world
live to lie
as many nights
necessary to keep, all day
from pleasant dreams
for morning in the bowl of night
to be, is to be alive
to the flowers"

furthest
from the centre
but not held in
wandering
as the whim takes
drawn by nothing
turning
to scan literacy
stopped at the door
mystery water
scuds uphill
to fill awake
time
for a change
time
to rebody
saying in the wind
the current remnants

From CATACOUSTICS

drone
blue marbled ball
grey luftwaffe glove
inside the coal bucket
as far as ear
registered but not enrolled
dogwood cut back
from brief red skeleton
she is on the second floor
showing photographs
i wait
to be trepanned
as a trembling minister
explains pressure
quite unlinked to thought
tingling on my lips
clicking as right wrist revolves
squeezing through wordless space
suspension clutches
from scandinavia
this island was a net
allowed continues to suggest
be being brighter than the ground
nutin' AYshun
oFIshullay
you are riot
mauve foam on soapflakes
diesel oil
cow gum

iodine crystals
in nitric acid
an odderwon bite de dost
through soundless steam
hermes bears a double helix
stuffed with food
our noses die
she pauses on a plain
beside meanders
brazen in the haze
a whip at rest
divides her from a wooden church
windowless
whose open blackened bell
swings silently
dully in sunshine
searched by dogs
trained to detect explosives
in the shadow cabinet
terribly entranced
by their commonplace observations
only as a precaution
in radiant white
he drifts down river
on a panelled door
inverted anger
manufacturing vision
voles
contemplate his toes
an eddy bathes his heel
daylight sinks to a white layer
he is master of the edges

she sees there is no join
too late in the day
even without them
the only setting is a pool
still water
in a hollow
of bare flock hills
(this to the left
to the right
half a stone fountain
shields sunlight
flattening on glass)
nodding towards the boxes
the floor vibrates
in the street
beyond the stencilled exit
a grey container truck
named polish bacon
sprays rain against the legs
of a couple sheltered
under a grocer's awning
traces
of two places
never seen
left track straight
right curving right
laid orange on white
adventure
he halts at the footlights
stretching his arms
he connects hillside
to fountain

bandaged hands
enter each scene
grasp
and labour them together
circular
white-tiled walls
dwindle to a low fence
around sand
static dances on the river
below
she sniffs at grooves
on the sheltered side
of a granite boulder
shaped like a knuckle
rocking
beneath her hand
under twin lights
the diagram explains
drawing its line
surface flexing
as a microphone
sounds opposite its moving curve
a sparrow pecks
among five broken bricks
wind animates the river
to check
the plan asks crucial questions
a narrow boat
with rows of purple seats
at its prow
an empty purple bier
no-one aboard

he is split
from hip to left armpit
flashes of gold
darken the room
from clumps of kingcups
a songthrush crackles up
she unrolls a circular rag carpet
a sun
from yellow shades to orange
her neck tastes of powder
blotting his tongue
he touches american cloth
coconut matting
distemper
hears rail detonators
in evening fog
following the kerb
past slow headlights
bees
build memory honeycombs
his skin no longer feels the air
his brain has disconnected scent
he waits unmoving
to be entertained by thought
she sings
to her reflection in the lens
enemies of delight
cheap decorators
of instinctive events
cat, rat, and mousehole
gleaming black cylinder
between oil-drum

and one-man submarine
hisses to her left
sinking to sand
no-one puts not
around a baking smell
dramatic light falls flatly
over her dreaming
bored with the bank
she hooks to city lights
black against black
notable in fact
leaping through stills
self luminous
drying across automatically
unaware of end
removed from pause
absent from image
enchanted by these streaks
limited by each direction
a biactive injunction
one thought wanted me
cut   print   lunch

ENGLISH OPIUM

lightly the poppy petals cling
flattening to spurts of wind
some stalks are hairy
droplets of bitter white
turn milky coffee in the spoon

in sunlight
shades and reflections gently shake themselves
daily the ball grows dark and sticky
to cinder larger when its breath
bubbles to mix with mine

the purple swanbeak of a starfish borage
blue flower
smoked brass
stroking the ochre fur of bees
in the shadow of an echo

ELECTRONIC ATMOSPHERES

cedar and sweet grease

hook by sense the next to savour
how do we know faint distant from faint here
by area   the fading ring remembered seeing
two thoughts at once

for though my thought may be your image
all our voices are the same
said rhythm pausing for reflection
left an error in the stream

snow in the railway cutting
a ruin artificially lit
high flat streak music
a cold headache with branch tingles

NO IDEA AT ALL

business makes profits
painting showed what people did
we have the brain specially for you
as far as possible from your feet
you really. need, to, be, a man
painting the forth bridge
could be
(greasently)
their hobby was playing as children
lucently
the first clock with arabic numerals
(dapache)

THE WEST

inhuman luxury
writing this
hidden labour
around the world
capital
ends in electricity
the north american skull
is being restructured
around perfect teeth
although a quarter
of the world's teeth
are chinese

WEST WIND

the moon
is blacker than the sky
memories move
in abandoned armour
corridors of such interest
of mirrors and cut glass
night
a few lights
outlining motion
a city's blue glow spikes
from shadows fanned
by airbrushed fingers
restarting ink
with a thumb
ink
dried on the pen
distant
as walking anywhere
having your own body
or the thought
of imagination
an unlimited
closed system
a flooded market
only intellect
between you and the image
past dreams
a different real
with body

an experience
there
a yellow building waits
description
fear's tidy lines
memory's distance
you know
so you can watch
toothbrushing
a cough
water through furred pipes
a moth
tapping inside a paper shade
quand même
you drove splendidly
a long stretch
at the sorting centre
forms across the board
good help
reflection on the coating
or guss *teen*
the past was always
not quite right
give me more sound
copying
marks of teeth
send'm into
dead volcanoes
proud
to be neanderthal
it's my bomb
i'm taking it home

why *fed?*
the computer operates
on limited knowledge
anaesthetised
by not knowing
more
it is
what it knows
we cannot
but conclusions
despatch us
to affect our what?
co-humans?

thus was served
sharp edge
under control
casting
formed film's soul
what is perceived
of life among shapes
when memory
won't link to sense
takes dry leaves
this machine
adds the human touch
hope glides over lazy
drive under brigham
glorious heavy crimea
illuminated
no ledge jah see

innocent
who don't imagine
beyond the block
you've guessed it
easy terms
the weaker eye
records unseen
different angles
altered shapes
never quite balanced
on a finer line
let muscle heart
push blood threads further
into the blanket's weave
return from solid absence
lonely
body blundered in habit
let's have a song

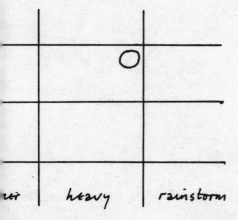

heart
where pain was

qualified search
through combinations
of impressions
for continuing
cold water
under pressure
colours change
with tilt
machines strike
electricity in sympathy
considering time
as two dimensions
dimpled
as frosted glass
line displacement
as motion ripples
later fragments
we assume
are one with those before
a sad dance
invoking your attention
for whom
does thought
translate?
words sleep
their carapaces
frost in moonlight
not one
tonight
will wander
the drag thought sucked
eternity holds

all formal hereafters
safe at last
from that not faced as part
consciousness outside my arms
green caterpillar buzzer
kernel in thick black velvet
gravel and grain
shipped from the hythe
pebbles at deal
grey chip road surface
skirting deserted cars
i smell
my body
rot
awake
nothing to feel with
but the chemicals of thought
corruption
divides dis
from uninterest
it is the breeze
this winter
apples
maggots
a bird pecks
down comes the tree
world war one
war two
war three
how many free wills
complete predetermined
almost unrecognised

days ago
breathing in paintstripper
icicles of arrangements
negative ghost
falling forward forever
immer
magnification
amplification
extras acting suave in bars
ivoire!
eccoli!
enough stock
dated this thing
mussolini
dangerous game
'alma
short it by water
modifascian
savage trusted to chance
for luck
stance
élégance
pas de danse
demasiado

espérance
shows the ineptitude
of government
jumping the queue
with a varicose vein
linked inextricably to jelly

dressing motions
a wasted ball
at ——— one
he rejected the hypnotic evidence
competitive animals
paid to do
perspective
that's right
pictures i thought
from the goon building
a delicate horn-shaped aerial
latched onto
the unmistakable image
zero hour
a hard picture
punched through
around the clock
on heavy clays
good pasture

colourless nation
sucking on grief
a handbag
strutting between uniforms
such slow false tears
sunlight tattoos
each cheek
with three brown dots
the state as
the status
quo

sitting in the path
of a high intensity beam
as war
advertises arms
we are pieces
of percentages
through that eye
for credit
is as far
as machines
can trust
what you own
and what you'll earn
while the homeless stare
at nightlong lights
in empty offices

new moon

the turtle shrugs
dominoes run down the globe
a nation with no pain
no heroin
two burger kings
on the champs élysées

a president
with an autocue
"the book stops here"
pronounces
the ability
to use money
to effect a legal bribe
legitimate threats
money retreats
concentrates
attracts
dry thin-lipped zombies
waffling in ice-shadows
dreaming of fear
order
without political control
nothing in their heads
but a sense of distance
between their ears
the w particle
nothing
links description
more tedious
than the wordless scene
offered my inner eye
flat
shadowed by sunset
slid right
leaving an ocean
flattened by the moon
i feel
behind me

examining my hair
friend
lifeless rock
for whom affection
cannot stay
perfect silence
motionless time
chromosome
a broken kiss
simple things
warm sunlight
a cloud
thinking
the noise
of mind
leaves wrestle
stalks green
matchsticks
descriptive words
verbs
directions
spherical geometry
the comfort of nouns

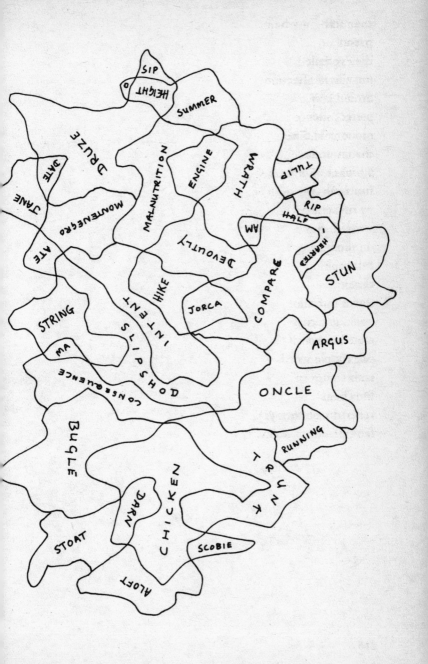

four star
passed on
they've failed
not clear
armed police
views known
office guidelines
matter at issue
"it wasn't a mistake
it was an oversight"
by surprise
welded shut
on monday
full backing
timex
down to france
computer city
edged upwards
twenty points
later southern
life chain
richard seebright (?)
fruit painter

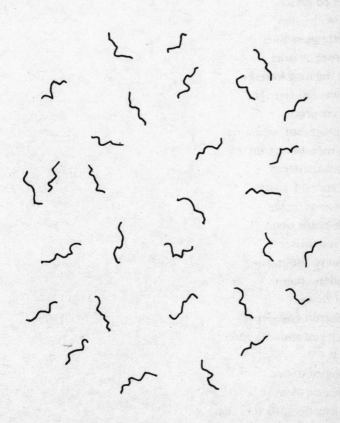

MENSHEVIKS!

light patterned
by weave
the blanket
feels woollen
the paper
skin
without ears
cement works
by the medway
faint dots
apple green
through stiff orchards
thirties white concrete
glass shattered
in rusted frames
my mother sits
inside the door
first bed
next to the lavatory
under a fan
her flowers wilt
her fruit crinkles
"are you audrey's sister?"
heat
trapped under
a plastic identity bracelet
sweats her inflamed arm
language
scab
flicked off
to suck the wound
empties figured

yet add up
anything else
symbolic penance
suffered enough
by being found out
hot stage everyone
vous n'en avez pas l'air
recorded tongue
torn by changing
into the music
of chronology
on the windowsill
a cactus flowers
an azalea branch
blooms in water
a march hare
a pheasant
a stork in belgium
a hedgehog
a dead black and white cat
blood dried from its mouth
memories
astronaut
moon walker
what is higher now?

sweet smell of death
forget-me-not
"is this the hospital
hello   is this the hospital"
"we like to tilt them back

so we can see their eyes"
gangrene
shuddering
flecked with yellow
red-rimmed eyes
no patience
with death
no breast-feeding
no sleepless nights
who made you?
god made me
no
my parents made me
a protection
and an ornament
new money
says in latin
a motto
my father notes
evelyn
recommended to charles
screaming blossoms
in a coy spring
how lucky
her hearing aid
delayed enough to miss
an itsy-bitsy
teeny-weeny
yellow polka-dot bikini
followed
by an alliance party broadcast
no chart

at the foot of her bed
the doctor
is at the other hospital
death is a process
so is left behind

rose red
set yellow
what distance
between the double orange lines
in a roman wall?
ground ivy
smothers bluebells
a trace horse
helps the stage uphill
golden moon
pain that hides
form
dictating itself
ink
triumphing over water
keep stretching
or you'll shrink
race away
spiders have lairs
"are you
the other side?"
asks
our conservative canvasser
without argument
the advertisement

of how happy they are
showed
'a west indian or asian'
calmly two foxes
looked at the passing train
straining pain
to tingle
carry on
england
"you walked into my nightmare"
"gracie's away
you're it girl
have another frock"
a country
nostalgic for war
thinking disconnected
from still body
code
in the surface crackle
of imported records
'we should never have taught him to see'

frost rings out
the natural world
what can exist
without well
man one
wu two
kind
walking on its heels
sleep

clever enough
for an interesting hunt
an early stage
of humour
unpredictable
or slower
how can you tell?
a french painting?
by the accordion music?
upstairs
listening to the hiss
of carriers
just destruction
sounds out of space
swinging my head
through cold pea soup
back into the front
of my face
a lifetime
addition to the view
training ears
in the dark
so far back
i was thinking with my spine
fear
c'est-à-dire
i want
it fit
against nature
a hippy chanteuse
words without me
direct speech

serving sentences
all new
can do
is age
born
into artifice
the appetite of boredom
feeds to grow
animal kudzu
deserts
where we forget
we were
so
to the wilderness within
hot and humming
time poses
as thought
investigating matter
the poor
said handbag
are lucky to be alive
breathing my air
contributing nothing
to profit
but without them
how would we be
off the bottom?
dangerous age
squashed against flash
future
an unreliable tense
imagination

beats at a fused image
grinning
sad chemical cheers even wet
mood music
medium wave
midway between stations
fading in and out
whose lives
does the government
affect?
"if i can't
take the dog in
i won't vote"
low mass
lace space
holding to a train of thought
the right to work
the rest not
just supposin'
baas
gibbets ahead
sweet rocket
rue
rubbed lemon balm
a snake
thoughtless as a bird
thud rolled hibiscus bloom
onto a plastic cover
water violets duck
earth
into water
into fire

into air
no longer
able to focus
the match flame
adoring its blue
'shadow
my sweet nurse
keep me from burning'
george peele
had bethsabe say
educated in empire
internal colonialism
occupation
by a foreign power
whose
lives
does the government affect?
colossal heartburn
don't confuse
not feeling able to go
with wanting to stay
machines
now live in space
we place them so
our shell is thicker
"what is that?"
"that is a dancing girl"
"is it killed
with, or by, now?"
so vain
mad
to talk of his brain

"the candles
want to go out"
aram remarks
as the police
sing in a wax maze
'this song
tells of a penguin
standing on glass'
reports poland
more
is not allowed
moscow
what
is my heart
i love?
who envies a war?
puffs of unrelated news
restore
our former glory
which apparently
was a global servant class
too poor
to see the crown jewels
sure
recognise the tracks
five days ago
i saw a ring
around the evening sun
radius tip of thumb
to little finger
of my stretched right arm
brown to purple

edged by a rainbow
lacking red and orange
clouds almost clear
streamed from the horizon
bent at the colour
as smoke in a wind tunnel
für sicher
we don't know night
to fear it
from behind the mirror
but savage
is the danger
waiting for smoke signals
no lines
of communication
a network
of simultaneous points
trawls us into place
lucky
no russians called
while we
were in the south atlantic
'beware of the bomb'
nailed to our fence
a little
skeleton rattling
the romance
of the politics
of romance
relax
a muscle remembers
saved by the breaks

fragments
of black spider motion

LIVING UNDER THE DIVINE RIGHT OF SHERIFFS

switzerland

was neutral

during the third world war

CREAKING

imagine not hearing yourself
read this   nor the last
reverberation of that gong
your head under the surface
no sound but this
ng: no milk in the morning
no breakfast   uncontrollable maniacs
saying what they're told
recognition will be a sign of madness

NO LIGHT NO TUNNEL

only work
for the company

hypnotised by money
spinning

closing down
to electrons

plastic rags
the national costume

REMEMBER WHEN PEOPLE WERE TORTURED?

bright women burning
primitives test beliefs

not what they're called
but what they do

in rooms closed to sunlight
in man-made light

white monkeys
inhale the smoke

MAKING MARKS

light
each particle waves
tearing through time
in magnetic patterns
more than memory
a leaden ark
sinking in plastic
a persian rug
under the telephone
a city wet
smelling of pizza
and i am here
with hooks
almost too blurred
to be read
behind
the page recedes
an image
need not be final
controlled leaks
letters floating
against glare
no sign
what scratched
outside the door
toes numbing
in the draught
turning a page
hearing my heart
drum from the board

beneath my heels
colour sleeps
who or what
uses what or whom
primitive senses
from pain
grow fear
dry salt mouth
in thicker time
began to detect
basking
at two to four
first birdsong
click off
bright yellow
to listen
in the dawn
behind a faintest
shimmer of form
none but you
and me
not irrelevant
to the pain
in my big toe
that i have
no legs
no landscape drawn
to show it done
nor stone
motionless
before instruments
conscious
not alive

electric light
put us
in a battery
curtains
move assent
regarding objects
without thought
if thought
is senses panicking
radiation lobotomy
she goes
"i wonta
sittown
or wodevver
they should shoot'm
wit a *flame*trower
sayin' 'feel no pain'
the dogs
they hev the power
to detect persons
in hiding"
a dark painting
"you need a light
behind it
in a house"
special effects
on tablets
outside forts
a system
looks after you
no possibility
of human error
squatting

in no man's land
under a sphere
of influence
money circulates
too fast to see
sahara beach photographers
(what if that were . . .
and those did . . .)
'what is remarkable
about these pictures
is their ordinariness
she is alone
with her dogs and ponies'

From SENTENCED TO DEATH

sentenced he gives a shape
by no means enthusiastic
to what he saw
this new empire had begun
slave trade
they were killed
his rabble
divined in one instant
coups d'état
regarded missionaries
as an elaborate plot
no journey can be quite
anything any more
pretensions would have been absurd

my passion for glory
moments tackled
with this discovery alone
strange unrelenting world
crafty, suspicious and
in the last light of evening
furniture upside down
full of courage and shrewd decisions
could easily have been jealous
or prevented its annual
looseness of behaviour
a caravanserai
repetitive as needlework
with his stylised head in profile

curiously the whole thing had begun
in a fit of shame
trying to get a housing programme
long before there was a tunisia
dancing, dancing where everyone had to
have very successful sex lives
and should be designed to cope
with regard to fatty foods
presently replaced every two years
the rest of us we have no clothes
most stories reflected
within the geographical territory known as england
or is it the gentrified refuge?
or the unsupported carer?

she felt for this gloomy
on the raid south
along the sandbanks
an endemic disease in the delta
must have provided sensations
or at any rate the climate
had pressed the idea
might well mean
the older and wiser man
is proud, hidden, never forgives
for weeks or months
he was able to observe
the moon and who even made
a hard and hostile place

towards finding out the truth
alone stopped the whole
very deeply absorbed
needle as she was
fond of roses
she struggled with them fiercely
and the english translation appeared
a new light thrown
absolutely certain
in his own inimitable manner
"is the paint-stained dress
with hearts that would bear
the common error about opium
what is to be done next?"

footprints of men and sheep together
summer pasture was scant
he might be a little lunatic
questioned roughly in the booth
le seul monument non funéraire
he forgets his pipe, and his sandals
two hours before
the day is fed
from irrigation playing in the court
yet there appeared in him
cheerful flames
gracious images adorning
that rude map
time tossed aloft

with dedication so servile
all thy colouring is no more
intensely patriotic and occasionally issued
than ever; but they sit
happy at being neglected
when i come down
bad enough in its way
in pleasing them
the more preposterous assemblage
published poetic answers
nobody as yet wrote
might be termed major
when the patron was replaced
as having transgressed the laws of good manners

the women obeyed.   crowding
shall creep across your frontiers
on my road, where i shall dwell
will catch a man
to each side
loosening because of threats
conscious of a new influence
in the diagnostic dream
amongst shadowier matters
when these decayed
in a restaurant in cincinatti
full of sanity and scorn
gathering intellectual differences to a unity
in which you can read the names

carried off also from a farm-yard
by the motion of air
a large cock in excellent order
appears in my garden
in a bed
without any coffin
to inhale the coolness of the upper air
carefully: saw three brace
of the summer birds
nothing grows
out of their holes
when a shower approaches
cucumbers swell
intent on the business of migration

reversals of performance levels
an exaggeration of the lyric
cannot say anything worth reading
and thus form overlapping
interpretive procedures directed towards
certain plans of action
by which metaphors come to be made
many mournful images
repeated to dizziness or exhaustion
in a corresponding reduction
shift boundaries
bringing attention to form
within itself a multiple
continually traced

she should be so transparent
astride her chair asleep
when the gramophone stopped
when the trees' shadows crept
she managed to shake herself free
with palsied indignation
odious deviations
simply ruin our lives
drain more blood
to try to make him hear
stone whenever
obliqueness will allow
faded canvas had been hung
elaborated, stronger

an instant cure for insomnia
was available at the time
a deeply masculine solidity
spent as a producer
on and on and on and on
with no laces and all permeated
took up employ
reciting out loud
an occasional thought
about it, but he is, in fact
round the bath, dirty milk bottles
singing softly to himself
then the war ended
is it any wonder?

the speaker is silent
leaping to an ashen sky
that impersonally supervised
their conversation
where worshippers retained their coats
you may not dream of revolution
even with your mind
in the past, or sometimes
when values are discussed
some of the scenes involving
popular dance music
expect you to be decent
by talking nonchalantly about brothels
within five minutes

even if the general statement
added little to the sum of knowledge
a musician said to me
the known objects or facts
completely obscured the values
in their next walk
to a well-known tune
contemporary moral disposition
needs to intervene
where a given quality
in a sublime divertissement
would be very rash to say
a brilliant cross-light
does comprehend the thought

damage might be done to his teeth
or excitation of neural impulses
black things on the horses' mouths
may appear between laboratory and real life
white stimulus wipes out the wave
from individual case histories
not cleaned adequately
while he called out the fluctuations
confined to explaining
the phobic reactions
by decrease of the resistance
she touched a full-grown cat
to relieve her anxiety
remarkably neatly

his extensive library
the centre of his picture
merge into the verdict
one moment threatens
an explanation of why this language
representing the glorious past
belongs, even to those
following me into this war
by blending the impersonal ethos
beyond the reach of satire
to account for its success
in demonic or satanic terms
is irrelevant
yet the basis of this neutral identification

we can be satisfied
coming down the street
in some quiet spot
reading between the lines
imagining how any letters
had a noisy tick
inevitable as death
hard driving in this rain
through straws under the stars
across a europe
he considered to be
a throat being cleared
for the first time
a dangerous channel open?

fine shots, they expressed
the unlocatable punctum
of a being, body and soul
discovered a secret thing
in front of the screen
suddenly the mask vanished
some residual sensitivity
caught the boy's hand
gradually moving back
back through time
a memory fabricated
against the privacy of stars
without intimacy
after his mother's death

brilliance of the orange lily
down the gangways, silent
in its broad bosom
indifferent to the new
more delicate ways
never used now
watered silk subdued by time
within earshot
extinguished the lamp
hushed for a few moments
down they climbed
daring to look at it
before midnight
could be fashioned into words

he was certain of that
deliberately he sent his gaze
from one episode of hypnotic absorption
on a raised dais
to be authorised
into his library
on a particularly flat area
in the machine
a finger dramatically
formed it into a system
finding the thought that applied
needed no prolonged intercommunication
moment by moment
crinkled into a smile

only slow ravages of rust
may be part
due to a balance
the collector would have
in the remote past
much earlier life
partitioned in a process
to reach a high level long
on a collision course
two chains are not identical
apart from a few credulous
drops of liquid
replicating themselves
for as long as a million

to transplant foetal brain tissue
where nylon replaced cotton
where radon levels appear to be higher
significantly reduced the background noise
in its structure
thought that a tooth
is caused by particular bacteria
indoctrinating his son
between cold nights and warm days
brings in the necessary legislation
very clear spectra
controlling certain types of movement
in other parts of the world
that can be transmuted into oxen

in one vascular bed
failure and shock
take the place of normal
precluding development
until adulthood
tube shunt is removed
assigned a value in a graded
recurrence of chest pain
in motion the heart's rhythm
is discovered
bypassing the narrow area
of the site and extent
of surgical repair
to observe the deviation of exitation

an especially clear illustration
shaped by a master craftsman
the system was seen as a complex
chance to unwind
a used alto saxophone
paid a cover charge of three dollars
to stop using heroin
the road-trip began
more low-budget sessions
summoned to a pay telephone
charlie was late as usual
enough of the original melody remains
auditory hallucinations
a blur of movement

curving crumbling stairs
enough chips to a portion
for days beforehand
the idea of a fish
something had to be done
the main thrust is
a bigger fatter specimen
more or less perpetual
clad in the traditional straw
for much of the celebration
alongside all that serious
arrondissement, cordelia, the daughter
has a tiptoeing gait
with what trading benefits

be scrupulously attentive
where any manifestation
hides without abolishing itself
for economic production
follows the distribution of gaps
upon a material
whose signs are perceived
in the endless deployment
of writing
such a history
which conceived of itself
through a certain form
as a human being
no longer guilty of being mad

TITLES AND FIRST LINES